D0845340

WITHDRAWN

The STRANGERS AND BROTHERS *novel-sequence*
by C. P. SNOW

STRANGERS AND BROTHERS

THE CONSCIENCE OF THE RICH

TIME OF HOPE

THE LIGHT AND THE DARK

THE MASTERS

THE NEW MEN

HOMECOMING

THE AFFAIR

CORRIDORS OF POWER

C. P. Snow is also the author of

THE SEARCH

VARIETY OF MEN

VARIETY
OF MEN

❖

C. P. SNOW

⚹ *New York* ⚹

CHARLES SCRIBNER'S SONS

TO MY SON

Philip

✦ Contents ✦

✦ *Preface* ✦

I SHOULD like this book to be read as a set of personal impressions, and no more than that. I have not included any bibliography of the sources I have consulted: that would be too portentous for what I set out to do. I have been interested in these men for a long time, and have read the standard works about them (and, in some cases, works less well known) as carefully as I can. All of them, with the exception of Rutherford and Stalin, themselves produced a certain amount of autobiographical material. That I have drawn on: though, of course, autobiographical material, even from people of introspective insight (such as Robert Frost, Hammarskjöld, Hardy) can be as misleading as any other, and needs just as critical an eye.

I met them all except Stalin, though Churchill only at committees, which didn't teach me much. My personal stories I can guarantee: these are the only parts of the book where I can say with certainty this—or something very like this—happened. I ought to make one qualification. I have reported a number of conversations in which I took part. When I report remarks in direct speech, I believe that my memory is accurate, and that they were said in those words, or in words closely similar. I have a pretty good memory, but not a freakish one. I have never met anyone who can totally recall a long conversation over a period of hours, much less of years. These remarks which stuck in my memory, and which I can vouch for, were usually said in the course of prolonged conversations. The rest has gone, or left only a general impression of its sense. By abstracting the words which most impressed or amused me, I may sometimes without intending to have introduced an emphasis of my own. I don't think I have, but I ought to give the warning. Even in the course of work as modest in intention as this, one realizes that accurate personal history is next door to impossible.

I have had to include a few explanations of where I was, and what I was doing, when I had these meetings—or, in some cases, these acquaintanceships and friendships. As I say in the piece on Wells, a novelist as a rule ought not to write an auto-biography, and I shall never do so. But it would have been arti-ficial in this book not to put in a sprinkling of autobiographical comments. It takes two to make a confrontation, whoever the two people are, even when it is Einstein receiving an unknown young man.

I wrote the book for fun, not because of the grandeur of most of my subjects, though of course that helped. The real fun was in the variety of human beings. That has been my chief pre-occupation ever since I can remember: even when, for a mixture of reasons, I have had to turn my attention to other things.

One final note. People sometimes think that, if one has had the luck to run across men of great achievement, they are likely to enter as characters into novels. That is quite wrong. The people who attract a novelist's imagination are usually not like that at all. They strike home, as it were, when one is not look-ing. In fact, of these men, Hardy did strike home, and he ap-pears, in a form so transmogrified that no one has ever noticed, in some of my books. If I had known Robert Frost when I was younger, I fancy that he might have tempted me in a similar fashion. But to contemplate Einstein for the purpose of fiction would be unimaginable. It is great luck to have known him and the others, but that is where it stops.

C.P.S.
Sept.29/66

VARIETY OF MEN

RUTHERFORD

IN 1923, at the meeting of the British Association for
the Advancement of Science in Liverpool, Rutherford
announced, at the top of his enormous voice: "We are
living in the heroic age of physics." He went on saying the
same thing, loudly and exuberantly, until he died, fourteen
years later.

The curious thing was, all he said was absolutely true.
There had never been such a time. The year 1932 was the
most spectacular year in the history of science. Living in
Cambridge, one could not help picking up the human, as
well as the intellectual, excitement in the air. James Chadwick, grey-faced after a fortnight of work with three
hours' sleep a night, telling the Kapitsa Club (to which
any young man was so proud to belong) how he had discovered the neutron; P. M. S. Blackett, the most handsome of men, not quite so authoritative as usual, because
it seemed too good to be true, showing plates which
demonstrated the existence of the positive electron; John
Cockcroft, normally about as much given to emotional

display as the Duke of Wellington, skimming down King's Parade and saying to anyone whose face he recognized: "We've split the atom! We've split the atom!"

It meant an intellectual climate different in kind from anything else in England at the time. The tone of science was the tone of Rutherford: magniloquently boastful—boastful because the major discoveries were being made—creatively confident, generous, argumentative, lavish, and full of hope. The tone differed from the tone of literary England as much as Rutherford's personality differed from that of T. S. Eliot. During the twenties and thirties Cambridge was the metropolis of experimental physics for the entire world. Even in the late nineteenth century, during the professorships of Clerk Maxwell and J. J. Thomson, it had never quite been that. "You're always at the crest of the wave," someone said to Rutherford. "Well, after all, I made the wave, didn't I?" Rutherford replied.

I remember seeing him a good many times before I first spoke to him. I was working on the periphery of physics at the time, and so didn't come directly under him. I already knew that I wanted to write novels, and that was how I should finish, and this gave me a kind of ambivalent attitude to the scientific world; but, even so, I could not avoid feeling some sort of excitement, or enhancement of interest, whenever I saw Rutherford walking down Free School Lane.

He was a big, rather clumsy man, with a substantial bay-window that started in the middle of the chest. I should guess that he was less muscular than at first sight he looked. He had large staring blue eyes and a damp and pendulous lower lip. He didn't look in the least like an intellectual. Creative people of his abundant kind never do, of course, but all the talk of Rutherford looking like a farmer was unperceptive nonsense. His was really the kind of face and physique that often goes with great weight of character and gifts. It could easily have been the soma of a great writer. As he talked to his companions in the street, his voice was three times as loud as any of theirs, and his accent was bizarre. In fact, he came from the very poor: his father was an odd-job man in New Zealand and the son of a Scottish emigrant. But there was nothing Antipodean or Scottish about Rutherford's accent; it sounded more like a mixture of West Country and Cockney.

In my first actual meeting with him, perhaps I could be excused for not observing with precision. It was early in 1930; I had not yet been elected a Fellow of my own college, and so had put in for the Stokes studentship at Pembroke. One Saturday afternoon I was summoned to an interview. When I arrived at Pembroke, I found that the short list contained only two, Philip Dee and me. Dee was called in first; as he was being interviewed, I was reflecting without pleasure that he was one of the brightest of Rutherford's bright young men.

Then came my turn. As I went in, the first person I saw, sitting on the right hand of the Master, was Rutherford himself. While the Master was taking me through my career, Rutherford drew at his pipe, not displaying any excessive interest in the proceedings. The Master came to the end of his questions, and said: "Professor Rutherford?"

Rutherford took out his pipe and turned on to me an eye which was blue, cold and bored. He was the most spontaneous of men; when he felt bored he showed it. That afternoon he felt distinctly bored. Wasn't his man, and a very good man, in for this job? What was this other fellow doing there? Why were we all wasting our time?

He asked me one or two indifferent questions in an irritated, impatient voice. What was my present piece of work? What could spectroscopy tell us anyway? Wasn't it just "putting things into boxes?"

I thought that was a bit rough. Perhaps I realized that I had nothing to lose. Anyway, as cheerfully as I could manage, I asked if he couldn't put up with a few of us not doing nuclear physics. I went on, putting a case for my kind of subject.

A note was brought round to my lodgings that evening. Dee had got the job. The electors wished to say that either candidate could properly have been elected. That sounded like a touch of Cambridge politeness, and I felt depressed. I cheered up a day or two later when I heard that Rutherford was trumpeting that I was a young man of spirit. Within a few months he backed me for another studentship. Incidentally, Dee was a far better scientist than I was or could have been, and neither Rutherford nor anyone else had been unjust.

From that time until he died, I had some opportunities of watching Rutherford at close quarters. Several of my friends knew him intimately, which I never did. It is a great pity that Tizard or Kapitsa, both acute psychological observers, did not write about him at length. But I belonged to a dining club which he attended, and I think I had serious conversations with him three times, the two of us alone together.

The difficulty is to separate the inner man from the Rutherfordiana, much of which is quite genuine. From behind a screen in a Cambridge tailor's, a friend and I heard a reverberating voice: "That shirt's too tight round the neck. Every day I grow in girth. *And* in mentality." Yet his physical make-up was more nervous than it seemed. In the same way, his temperament, which seemed exuberantly powerful, massively simple, rejoicing with childish satisfaction in creation and fame, was not quite so simple as all that. His was a personality of Johnsonian scale. As with Johnson, the façade was overbearing and unbroken. But there were fissures within.

No one could have enjoyed himself more, either in creative work or the honors it brought him. He worked hard, but with immense gusto; he got pleasure not only from the high moments, but also from the hours of what to others would be drudgery, sitting in the dark counting the alpha particle scintillations on the screen. His insight was direct, his intuition, with one curious exception, infallible. No scientist has made fewer mistakes. In the corpus of his published work, one of the largest in scientific history, there was nothing he had to correct afterwards. By thirty he had already set going the science of nuclear physics—single-handed, as a professor on five hundred pounds a year, in the isolation of late-Victorian Montreal. By forty, now in Manchester, he had found the structure of the atom—on which all modern nuclear physics depends.

It was an astonishing career, creatively active until the month he died. He was born very poor, as I have said.

New Zealand was, in the 1880's, the most remote of provinces, but he managed to get a good education; enough of the old Scottish tradition had percolated there, and he won all the prizes. He was as original as Einstein, but unlike Einstein he did not revolt against formal instruction; he was top in classics as well as in everything else. He started research—on the subject of wireless waves —with equipment such as one might rustle up today in an African laboratory. That did not deter him: "I could do research at the North Pole," he once proclaimed, and it was true. Then he was awarded one of the 1851 overseas scholarships (which later brought to England Florey, Oliphant, Philip Bowden, a whole series of gifted Antipodeans). In fact, he got the scholarship only because another man, placed above him, chose to get married: with the curious humility that was interwoven with his boastfulness, he was grateful all of his life. There was a proposal, when he was Lord Rutherford, President of the Royal Society, the greatest of living experimental scientists, to cut down these scholarships. Rutherford was on the committee. He was too upset to speak: at last he blurted out:

"If it had not been for them, I shouldn't have been." That was nonsense. Nothing could have stopped him. He brought his wireless work to Cambridge, anticipated Marconi, and then dropped it because he saw a field—radioactivity—more scientifically interesting.

If he had pushed on with wireless, incidentally, he couldn't have avoided becoming rich. But for that he never had time to spare. He provided for his wife and daughter, they lived in comfortable middle-class houses, and that was all. His work led directly to the atomic energy industry spending, within ten years of his death, thousands of millions of pounds. He himself never earned, or wanted to earn, more than a professor's salary—about £1,600 a year at the Cavendish in the thirties. In his will he left precisely the value of his Nobel Prize, then worth £7,000. Of the people I am writing about, he died much the poorest *: even G. H. Hardy, who by Rutherford's side looked so ascetic and unworldly, happened not to be above taking an interest in his investments.

As soon as Rutherford got on to radioactivity, he was set on his life's work. His ideas were simple, rugged, material: he kept them so. He thought of atoms as though they were tennis balls. He discovered particles smaller than atoms, and discovered how they moved or bounced. Sometimes the particles bounced the wrong way. Then he inspected the facts and made a new but always simple picture. In that way he moved, as certainly as a sleepwalker, from unstable radioactive atoms to the discovery of the nucleus and the structure of the atom.

In 1919 he made one of the significant discoveries of all time: he broke up a nucleus of nitrogen by a direct hit from an alpha particle. That is, man could get inside the atomic nucleus and play with it if he could find the right projectiles. These projectiles could either be provided by radioactive atoms or by ordinary atoms speeded up by electrical machines.

The rest of that story leads to the technical and military history of our time. Rutherford himself never built the great machines which have dominated modern parti-

* One has to leave Stalin out of this comparison.

cle physics, though some of his pupils, notably Cockcroft, started them. Rutherford himself worked with bizarrely simple apparatus: but in fact he carried the use of such apparatus as far as it would go. His researches remain the last supreme single-handed achievement in fundamental physics. No one else can ever work there again—in the old Cavendish phrase—with sealing wax and string.

It was not done without noise: it was done with anger and storms—but also with an overflow of creative energy, with abundance and generosity, as though research were the easiest and most natural avocation in the world. He had deep sympathy with the creative arts, particularly literature; he read more novels than most literary people manage to do. He had no use for critics of any kind. He felt both suspicion and dislike of the people who invested scientific research or any other branch of creation with an aura of difficulty, who used long, methodological words to explain things which he did perfectly by instinct. "Those fellows," he used to call them. "Those fellows" were the logicians, the critics, the metaphysicians. They were clever; they were usually more lucid than he was; in argument against them he often felt at a disadvantage. Yet somehow they never produced a serious piece of work, whereas he was the greatest experimental scientist of the age.

I have heard larger claims made for him. I remember one discussion in particular, a year or two after his death, by half-a-dozen men, all of whom had international reputations in science. Darwin was there: G. I. Taylor: Fowler and some others. Was Rutherford the greatest experimental scientist since Michael Faraday? Without any doubt.

Greater than Faraday? Possibly so. And then—it is interesting, as it shows the anonymous Tolstoyan nature of organized science—how many years' difference would it have made if he had never lived? How much longer before the nucleus would have been understood as we now understand it? Perhaps ten years. More likely only five.

Rutherford's intellect was so strong that he would, in the long run, have accepted that judgment. But he would not have liked it. His estimate of his own powers was realistic, but if it erred at all, it did not err on the modest side. "There is no room for this particle in the atom as designed by *me*," I once heard him assure a large audience. It was part of his nature that, stupendous as his work was, he should consider it 10 per cent more so. It was also part of his nature that, quite without acting, he should behave constantly as though he were 10 per cent larger than life. Worldly success? He loved every minute of it: flattery, titles, the company of the high official world. He said in a speech: "As I was standing in the drawing-room at Trinity, a *clergyman* came in. And I said to him: 'I'm Lord Rutherford.' And he said to me: 'I'm the Archbishop of York.' And I don't suppose either of us believed the other."

He was a great man, a very great man, by any standards which we can apply. He was not subtle: but he was clever as well as creatively gifted, magnanimous (within the human limits) as well as hearty. He was also superbly and magnificently vain as well as wise—the combination is commoner than we think when we are young. He enjoyed a life of miraculous success. On the whole he enjoyed his own personality. But I am sure that, even quite late in his life, he felt stabs of a sickening insecurity.

Somewhere at the roots of that abundant and creative nature there was a painful, shrinking nerve. One has only to read his letters as a young man to discern it. There are passages of self-doubt which are not to be explained completely by a humble colonial childhood and youth. He was uncertain in secret, abnormally so for a young man of his gifts. He kept the secret as his personality flowered and hid it. But there was a mysterious diffidence behind it all. He hated the faintest suspicion of being patronized, even when he was a world figure. Archbishop Lang was once tactless enough to suggest that he supposed a famous scientist had no time for reading. Rutherford immediately felt that he was being regarded as an ignorant roughneck. He produced a formidable list of his last month's reading. Then, half innocently, half malevolently: "And what do you manage to read, your Grice?" "I am afraid," said the Archbishop, somewhat out of his depth, "that a man in my position really doesn't have the leisure. . . ." "Ah, yes, your Grice," said Rutherford in triumph, "it must be a dog's life! It must be a dog's life!"

Once I had an opportunity of seeing that diffidence face to face. In the autumn of 1934 I published my first novel, which was called *The Search* and the background of which was the scientific world. Not long after it came out, Rutherford met me in King's Parade. "What have you been doing to us, young man?" he asked vociferously. I began to describe the novel, but it was not necessary; he announced that he had read it with care. He went on to invite, or rather command, me to take a stroll with him round the Backs. Like most of my scientific friends, he was good-natured about the book, which has some descriptions of the scientific experience which are probably somewhere near the truth. He praised it. I was gratified. It was a sunny October afternoon. Suddenly he said: "I didn't like the erotic bits. I suppose it's because we belong to different generations."

The book, I thought, was reticent enough. I did not know how to reply.

In complete seriousness and simplicity, he made another suggestion. He hoped that I was not going to write all my novels about scientists. I assured him that I was not—certainly not another for a long time.

He nodded. He was looking gentler than usual, and thoughtful. "It's a small world, you know," he said. He meant the world of science. "Keep off us as much as you can. People are bound to think that you are getting at some of us. And I suppose we've all got things that we don't want anyone to see."

I mentioned that his intuitive foresight went wrong just once. As a rule, he was dead right about the practical applications of science, just as much as about the nucleus. But his single boss shot sounds ironic now. In 1933 he said, in another address to the British Association, "These transformations of the atom are of extraordinary interest to scientists, but we cannot control atomic energy to an extent which would be of any value commercially, and I believe we are not likely ever to be able to do so. A lot of nonsense has been talked about transmutations. Our interest in the matter is purely scientific."

That statement, which was made only nine years before the first pile worked, was not intended to be either optimistic or pessimistic. It was just a forecast, and it was wrong.

That judgment apart, people outside the scientific world often felt that Rutherford and his kind were optimistic—optimistic right against the current of the twentieth century literary-intellectual mood, offensively and brazenly optimistic. This feeling was not quite unjustified, but the difference between the scientists and the non-scientists was more complex than that. When the scientists talked of the individual human condition, they did not find it any more hopeful than the rest of us. Does anyone really imagine that Bertrand Russell, G. H. Hardy, Rutherford, Blackett and the rest were bemused by cheerfulness as they faced their own individual state? Very few of them had any of the consolations of religion: they believed, with the same certainty that they believed in Rutherford's atom, that they were going, after this mortal life, into annihilation. Several of them were men of deep introspective insight. They did not need teaching anything at all about the existential absurdity.

Nevertheless it is true that, of the kinds of people I have lived among, the scientists were much the happiest. Somehow scientists were buoyant at a time when other intellectuals could not keep away despair. The reasons for this are not simple. Partly, the nature of scientific activity, its complete success on its own terms, is itself a source of happiness; partly, people who are drawn to scientific activity tend to be happier in temperament than other clever men. By the nature of their vocation and also by the nature of their own temperament, the scientists did not think constantly of the individual human predicament. Since they could not alter it, they let it alone. When they thought about people, they thought most of what could be altered, not what couldn't. So they gave their minds not to the individual condition but to the social one.

There, science itself was the greatest single force for change. The scientists were themselves part of the deepest revolution in human affairs since the discovery of agriculture. They could accept what was happening, while other intellectuals shrank away. They not only accepted it, they rejoiced in it. It was difficult to find a scientist who did not believe that the scientific-technical-industrial revolution, accelerating under his eyes, was not doing incomparably more good than harm.

This was the characteristic optimism of scientists in the twenties and thirties. Is it still? In part, I think so. But there has been a change.

In the Hitler war, physicists became the most essential of military resources: radar, which occupied thousands of physicists on both sides, altered the shape of the war, and the nuclear bomb finished large scale "conventional" war for ever. To an extent, it had been foreseen by the mid-thirties that if it came to war (which a good many of us expected) physicists would be called on from the start. Tizard was a close friend of Rutherford's, and kept him informed about the prospects of RDF (as radar was then called). By 1938 a number of the Cavendish physicists had been secretly indoctrinated. But no one, no one at all, had a glimmering of how, for a generation afterwards, a high percentage of all physicists in the

United States, the Soviet Union, this country, would remain soldiers-not-in-uniform. Mark Oliphant said sadly,
when the first atomic bomb was dropped: "This has killed
a beautiful subject." Intellectually that has turned out not
to be true: but morally there is something in it. Secrecy,
national demands, military influence, have sapped the
moral nerve of physics. It will be a long time before the
climate of Cambridge, Copenhagen, Göttingen in the
twenties is restored: or before any single physicist can speak
to all men with the calm authority of Einstein or Bohr.
That kind of leadership has now passed to the biologists,
who have so far not been so essential to governments. It
will be they, I think, who are likely to throw up the great
scientific spokesmen of the next decades. If someone now
repeated Gorki's famous question, "Masters of culture,
which side are you on?" it would probably be a biologist
who spoke out for his fellow human beings.

In Rutherford's scientific world, the difficult choices
had not yet formed themselves. The liberal decencies were
taken for granted. It was a society singularly free from
class or national or racial prejudice. Rutherford called
himself alternatively conservative or non-political, but
the men he wanted to have jobs were those who could do
physics. Niels Bohr, Otto Hahn, Georg von Hevesy, Hans
Geiger were men and brothers, whether they were Jews,
Germans, Hungarians—men and brothers whom he would
much rather have near him than the Archbishop of
Canterbury or one of "those fellows" or any damned English philosopher. It was Rutherford who, after 1933, took
the lead in opening English academic life to Jewish refugees. In fact, scientific society was wide open, as it may

not be again for many years. There was coming and going among laboratories all over the world, including Russia. Peter Kapitsa, Rutherford's favorite pupil, contrived to be in good grace with the Soviet authorities and at the same time a star of the Cavendish.

He had a touch of genius: in those days, before life sobered him, he had also a touch of the inspired Russian clown. He loved his own country, but he distinctly enjoyed backing both horses, working in Cambridge and taking his holidays in the Caucasus. He once asked a friend of mine if a foreigner could become an English peer; we strongly suspected that his ideal career would see him established simultaneously in the Soviet Academy of Sciences and as Rutherford's successor in the House of Lords.

At that time Kapitsa attracted a good deal of envy, partly because he could do anything with Rutherford. He called Rutherford "the Crocodile," explaining the crocodile means "father" in Russian, which it doesn't, quite: he had Eric Gill carve a crocodile on his new laboratory. He flattered Rutherford outrageously, and Rutherford loved it. Kapitsa could be as impertinent as a Dostoevskian comedian: but he had great daring and scientific insight. He established the club named after him (which again inspired some envy): it met every Tuesday night, in Kapitsa's rooms in Trinity, and was deliberately kept small, about thirty, apparently because Kapitsa wanted to irritate people doing physical subjects he disapproved of. We used to drink large cups of milky coffee immediately after hall (living was fairly simple, and surprisingly non-alcoholic, in scientific Cambridge), and someone gave a talk—often a dramatic one, like Chadwick's on the neutron. Several of the major discoveries of the thirties were first heard in confidence in that room. I don't think that the confidence was ever broken.

I myself enjoyed the one tiny scientific triumph of my life there. At the time Kapitsa barely tolerated me, since I did spectroscopy, a subject he thought fit only for bank clerks: in fact I had never discovered why he let me join. One night I offered to give a paper outside my own subject, on nuclear spin, in which I had been getting interested: I didn't know much about it, but I reckoned that most of the Cavendish knew less. The offer was unenthusiastically accepted. I duly gave the paper. Kapitsa looked at me with his large blue eyes, with a somewhat unflattering astonishment, as at a person of low intelligence who had contrived inadvertently to say something interesting. He turned to Chadwick, and said incredulously, "Jimmy, I believe there *is* something in this."

It was a personal loss to Rutherford when Kapitsa, on one of his holiday trips to Russia, was told by the Soviet bosses, politely but unyieldingly, that he must stay: he was too valuable, they wanted his services full-time. After a while Kapitsa made the best of it. He had always been a patriotic Russian: though both he and his wife came from the upper middle-class, if there was such a class in old Russia (his father was a general in the Tsarist engineering corps), he took a friendly attitude to the revolution. All that remained steady, though I don't think he would mind my saying that his enthusiasm for Stalin was not unqualified. Still, Kapitsa threw all his gifts into his new work in the cause of Soviet science. It was only then that we, who had known him in Cambridge, realized how strong a character he was: how brave he was: and fundamentally what a good man. His friendship with Cockcroft and others meant that the link between Soviet and English science was never quite broken, even in the worst days. Only great scientists like Lev Landau can say in full what he has done for science in his own country. If he hadn't existed, the world would have been worse: that is an epitaph that most of us would like and don't deserve.

Between Leningrad and Cambridge, Kapitsa oscillated. Between Copenhagen and Cambridge there was a stream of travellers, all the nuclear physicists of the world. Copenhagen had become the second scientific metropolis on account of the personal influence of one man, Niels Bohr, who was complementary to Rutherford as a person—patient, reflective, any thought hedged with Proustian qualifications—just as the theoretical quantum physics of which he was the master was complementary to Rutherford's experimental physics. He had been a pupil of Rutherford's, and they loved and esteemed each other like father and son. (Rutherford was a paterfamilias born, and the death of his only daughter seems to have been the greatest sorrow of his personal life. In his relations with Bohr and Kapitsa and others, there was a strong vein of paternal emotion diverted from the son he never had.) But, strong as Rutherford's liking for Bohr was, it was not strong enough to put up with Bohr's idea of a suitable length for a lecture. In the Cavendish lecture room, Bohr went past the hour; Rutherford began to stir. Bohr went past the hour and a half; Rutherford began plucking at his sleeve and muttering in a stage whisper about "another five minutes." Blandly, patiently, determined not to leave a qualification unsaid, as indefatigable as Henry James in his last period, Bohr went past the two hours; Rutherford was beginning to trumpet about "bringing the lecture to a close." Soon they were both on their feet at once.

Rutherford died suddenly when he was age sixty-six, still in full vigor. He died not only suddenly, but of something like a medical accident: he had a strangulated hernia. There was no discernible reason why he should not have lived into old age.

It was a sunny, tranquil October morning, the kind of day on which Cambridge looks so beautiful. I had just arrived at the crystallographic laboratory, one of the buildings in the old Cavendish muddle; why I was there I don't remember, nor whom I was talking to, except that it happened not to be Bernal. Someone put his head round the door and said: "The Professor's dead."

I don't think anyone said much more. We were stupefied rather than miserable. It did not seem in the nature of things.

G. H. HARDY

I T was a perfectly ordinary night at Christ's high table, except that Hardy was dining as a guest. He had just returned to Cambridge as Sadleirian professor, and I had heard something of him from young Cambridge mathematicians. They were delighted to have him back: he was a *real* mathematician, they said, not like those Diracs and Bohrs the physicists were always talking about: he was the purest of the pure. He was also unorthodox, eccentric, radical, ready to talk about anything. This was 1931, and the phrase was not yet in English use, but in later days they would have said that in some indefinable way he had star quality.

So, from lower down the table, I kept studying him. He was then in his early fifties: his hair was already grey, above skin so deeply sunburnt that it stayed a kind of Red Indian bronze. His face was beautiful—high cheek bones, thin nose, spiritual and austere but capable of dissolving into convulsions of internal gamin-like amusement. He had opaque brown eyes, bright as a bird's—a kind of eye not uncommon among those with a gift for conceptual thought. Cambridge at that time was full of unusual and distinguished faces—but even then, I thought that night, Hardy's stood out.

I do not remember what he was wearing. It may very easily have been a sports coat and grey flannels under his gown. Like Einstein, he dressed to please himself: though, unlike Einstein, he diversified his casual clothing by a taste for expensive silk shirts.

As we sat round the combination-room table, drinking wine after dinner, someone said that Hardy wanted to talk to me about cricket. I had been elected only a year before, but Christ's was then a small college, and the pastimes of even the junior fellows were soon identified. I was taken to sit by him. I was not introduced. He was, as I later discovered, shy and self-conscious in all formal actions, and had a dread of introductions. He just put his head down, as it were in a butt of acknowledgment, and without any preamble whatever began:

"You're supposed to know something about cricket, aren't you?"

Yes, I said, I knew a bit.

Immediately he began to put me through a moderately stiff viva. Did I play? What sort of performer was I? I half-guessed that he had a horror of persons, then prevalent in academic society, who devotedly studied the literature but had never played the game. I trotted out my credentials, such as they were. He appeared to find the reply partially reassuring, and went on to more tactical questions. Whom should I have chosen as captain for the last test match a year before (in 1930)? If the selectors had decided that Snow was the man to save England, what would have been my strategy and tactics? ("You are allowed to act, if you are sufficiently modest, as non-playing captain.") And so on, oblivious to the rest of the table. He was quite absorbed.

As I had plenty of opportunities to realize in the future, Hardy had no faith in intuitions or impressions, his own or anyone else's. The only way to assess someone's knowledge, in Hardy's view, was to examine him. That went for mathematics, literature, philosophy, politics, anything you like. If the man had bluffed and then wilted under the questions, that was his lookout. First things came first, in that brilliant and concentrated mind.

That night in the combination-room, it was necessary to discover whether I should be tolerable as a cricket companion. Nothing else mattered. In the end he smiled with immense charm, with child-like openness, and said that Fenner's (the university cricket ground) next season might be bearable after all, with the prospect of some reasonable conversation.

Thus, just as I owed my acquaintanceship with Lloyd George to his passion for phrenology, I owed my friendship with Hardy to having wasted a disproportionate amount of my youth on cricket. I don't know what the moral is. But it was a major piece of luck for me. This was intellectually the most valuable friendship of my life. His mind, as I have just mentioned, was brilliant and concentrated: so much so that by his side anyone else's seemed a little muddy, a little pedestrian and confused. He wasn't a great genius, as Einstein and Rutherford were. He said, with his usual clarity, that if the word meant anything he was not a genius at all. At his best, he said, he was for a short time the fifth best pure mathematician in the world. Since his character was as beautiful and candid as his mind, he always made the point that his friend and collaborator Littlewood was an appreciably more powerful mathematician than he was, and that his protégé Ramanujan really had natural genius in the sense (though not to the extent, and nothing like so effectively) that the greatest mathematicians had it.

People sometimes thought he was under-rating himself, when he spoke of these friends. It is true that he was magnanimous, as free from envy as a man can be: but I think one mistakes his quality if one doesn't accept his judgment. I prefer to believe in his own statement in *A Mathematician's Apology*, at the same time so proud and so humble:

> I still say to myself when I am depressed and find myself forced to listen to pompous and tiresome people, "Well, I have done one thing you could never have done, and that is to have collaborated with both Littlewood and Ramanujan on something like equal terms."

In any case, his precise ranking must be left to the historians of mathematics (though it will be an almost impossible job, since so much of his best work was done in collaboration). There is something else, though, at which he was clearly superior to Einstein or Rutherford or any other great genius: and that is at turning any work of the intellect, major or minor or sheer play, into a work of art. It was that gift above all, I think, which made him, almost without realizing it, purvey such intellectual delight.

When *A Mathematician's Apology* was first published, Graham Greene in a review wrote that along with Henry James's notebooks, this was the best account of what it was like to be a *creative artist*. Thinking about the effect Hardy had on all those round him, I believe that is the clue.

He was born, in 1877, into a modest professional family. His father was Bursar and Art Master at Cranleigh, then a minor public (English for private) school. His mother had been senior mistress at the Lincoln Training College for teachers. Both were gifted and mathematically inclined. In his case, as in that of most mathematicians, the gene pool doesn't need searching for. Much of his childhood, unlike Einstein's, was typical of a future mathematician's. He was demonstrating a formidably high I.Q. as soon as, or before, he learned to talk. At the age of two he was writing down numbers up to millions (a common sign of mathematical ability). When he was taken to church he amused himself by factorizing the numbers of the hymns: he played with numbers from that time on, a habit which led to the touching scene at Ramanujan's sick-bed: the scene is well known, but later on I shall not be able to resist repeating it.

It was an enlightened, cultivated, highly literate Victorian childhood. His parents were probably a little obsessive, but also very kind. Childhood in such a Victorian family was as gentle a time as anything we could provide, though probably intellectually somewhat more exacting. His was unusual in just two respects. In the first place, he suffered from an acute self-consciousness at an unusually early age, long before he was twelve. His parents knew he was prodigiously clever, and so did he. He came top of his class, he had to go in front of the school to receive prizes: and that he could not bear. Dining with me one night, he said that he deliberately used to try to get his answers wrong so as to be spared this intolerable ordeal. His capacity for dissimulation, though, was always minimal: he got the prizes all the same.

Some of this self-consciousness wore off. He became competitive. As he says in the *Apology*: "I do not remember having felt, as a boy, any *passion* for mathematics, and such notions as I may have had of the career of a mathematician were far from noble. I thought of mathematics in terms of examinations and scholarships: I wanted to beat other boys, and this seemed to be the way in which I could do so most decisively." Nevertheless, he had to live with an over-delicate nature. He seems to have been born with three skins too few. Unlike Einstein, who had to subjugate his powerful ego in the study of the external world before he could attain his moral stature, Hardy had to strengthen an ego which wasn't much protected. This at times in later life made him self-assertive (as Einstein never was) when he had to take a moral stand. On the other hand, it gave him his introspective insight and beautiful candor, so that he could speak of himself with absolute simplicity (as Einstein never could).

I believe this contradiction, or tension, in his temperament was linked with a curious tic in his behavior. He was the classical anti-narcissist. He could not endure having his photograph taken: so far as I know, there are not half-a-dozen photographs in existence. He would not have any looking-glass in his rooms, not even a shaving mirror. When he went to a hotel, his first action was to cover all the looking-glasses with towels. This would have been odd enough, if his face had been like a gargoyle: superficially it might seem odder, since all his life he was good-looking quite out of the ordinary. But, of course, narcissism and anti-narcissism have nothing to do with looks as outside observers see them.

This behavior seems eccentric, and indeed it was. Between him and Einstein, though, there was a difference in kind. Those who spent much time with Einstein—such as Infeld—found him grow stranger, less like themselves, the longer they knew him. I am certain that I should have felt the same. With Hardy the opposite was true. His behavior was often different, bizarrely so, from ours: but it came to seem a kind of superstructure set upon a nature which wasn't all that different from our own, except that it was more delicate, less padded, finer-nerved.

The other unusual feature of his childhood was more mundane: but it meant the removal of all practical obstacles throughout his entire career. Hardy, with his limpid honesty, would have been the last man to be finicky on this matter. He knew what privilege meant, and he knew that he had possessed it. His family had no money, only a schoolmaster's income, but they were in touch with the best educational advice of late nineteenth century England. That particular kind of information has always been more significant in this country than any amount of wealth. The scholarships have been there all right, if one knew how to win them. There was never the slightest chance of the young Hardy being lost—as there was of the young Wells or the young Einstein. From the age of twelve he had only to survive, and his talents would be looked after.

At twelve, in fact, he was given a scholarship at Winchester, then and for long afterwards the best mathematical school in England, simply on the strength of some mathematical work he had done at Cranleigh. (Incidentally, one wonders if any great school could be so elastic nowadays.) There he was taught mathematics in a class of one: in classics he was as good as the other top collegers. Later, he admitted that he had been well educated, but he admitted it reluctantly. He disliked the school, except for its classes. Like all Victorian public schools, Winchester was a pretty rough place. He nearly died one winter. He envied Littlewood in his cared-for home going as a day boy at St. Paul's and other friends at our free-and-easy grammar schools. He never went near Winchester after he had left it: but he left it, with the inevitability of one who had got on to the right tramlines, with an open scholarship to Trinity.

He had one curious grievance against Winchester. He was a natural ball-games player with a splendid eye. In his fifties he could usually beat the university second string at real tennis, and in his sixties I saw him bring off startling shots in the cricket nets. Yet he had not had an hour's coaching at Winchester: his method was defective: if he had been coached, he thought, he would have been a really good batsman, not quite first-class, but not too far away. Like all his judgments on himself, I believe that one is quite true. It is strange that, at the zenith of Victorian games-worship, such a talent was utterly missed. I suppose no one thought it worth looking for in the school's top scholar, so frail and sickly, so defensively shy.

It would have been natural for a Wykehamist of his period to go to New College. That wouldn't have made much difference to his professional career (though, since he always liked Oxford better than Cambridge, he might have stayed there all his life, and some of us would have missed a treat). He decided to go to Trinity instead, for a reason that he describes, humorously but with his usual undecorated truth, in the *Apology*. "I was about fifteen when (in a rather odd way) my ambitions took a sharper turn. There is a book by 'Alan St. Aubyn' (actually Mrs. Frances Marshall) called *A Fellow of Trinity*, one of a series dealing with what is supposed to be Cambridge college life. . . . There are two heroes, a primary hero called Flowers, who is almost wholly good, and a secondary hero, a much weaker vessel, called Brown. Flowers and Brown find many dangers in university life. . . . Flowers survives all these troubles, is Second Wrangler and succeeds automatically to a Fellowship (as I suppose he would have done then). Brown succumbs, ruins his parents, takes to drink, is saved from delirium tremens during a thunderstorm only by the prayers of the Junior Dean, has much difficulty in obtaining even an Ordinary Degree, and ultimately becomes a missionary. The friendship is not shattered by these unhappy events, and Flowers's thoughts stray to Brown, with affectionate pity, as he drinks port and eats walnuts for the first time in Senior Combination Room.

G. H. Hardy ⋈ 29

Now Flowers was a decent enough fellow (so far as "Alan St. Aubyn" could draw one), but even my unsophisticated mind refused to accept him as clever. If he could do these things, why not I? In particular, the final scene in Combination Room fascinated me completely, and from that time, until I obtained one, mathematics meant to me primarily a Fellowship of Trinity.

Which he duly obtained, after getting the highest place in the Mathematical Tripos Part II, at the age of twenty-two. On the way, there were two minor vicissitudes. The first was theological, in the high Victorian manner. Hardy had decided—I think before he left Winchester—that he did not believe in God. With him, this was a black-and-white decision, as sharp and clear as all other concepts in his mind. Chapel at Trinity was compulsory. Hardy told the Dean, no doubt with his own kind of shy certainty, that he could not conscientiously attend. The Dean, who must have been a jack-in-office, insisted that Hardy should write to his parents and tell them so. They were orthodox religious people, and the Dean knew, and Hardy knew much more, that the news would give them pain—pain such as we, seventy years later, cannot easily imagine.

Hardy struggled with his conscience. He wasn't worldly enough to slip the issue. He wasn't even worldly enough—he told me one afternoon at Fenner's, for the wound still rankled—to take the advice of more sophisticated friends such as George Trevelyan and Desmond MacCarthy, who would have known how to handle the matter. In the end he wrote the letter. Partly because of that incident, his religious disbelief remained open and active ever after. He refused to go into any college chapel even for formal business, like electing a master. He had clerical friends, but God was his personal enemy. In all this there was an echo of the nineteenth century: but one would be wrong, as always with Hardy, not to take him at his word.

Still, he turned it into high jinks. I remember, one day in the thirties, seeing him enjoy a minor triumph. It happened in a Gentlemen v. Players match at Lord's. It was early in the morning's play, and the sun was shining over the pavilion. One of the batsmen, facing the Nursery end, complained that he was unsighted by a reflection from somewhere unknown. The umpires, puzzled, padded round by the sight-screen. Motor-cars? No. Windows? None on that side of the ground. At last, with justifiable triumph, an umpire traced the reflection down—it came from a large pectoral cross reposing on the middle of an enormous clergyman. Politely the umpire asked him to take it off. Close by, Hardy was doubled up in Mephistophelian delight. That lunch time, he had no leisure for eating: he was writing postcards (postcards and telegrams were his favorite means of communication) to each of his clerical friends.

But in his war against God and God's surrogates, victory was not all on one side. On a quiet and lovely May evening at Fenner's, round about the same period, the chimes of six o'clock fell across the ground. "It's rather unfortunate," said Hardy simply, "that some of the happiest hours of my life should have been spent within sound of a Roman Catholic church."

The second minor upset of his undergraduate years was professional. Almost since the time of Newton, and all through the nineteenth century, Cambridge had been dominated by the examination for the old Mathematical Tripos. The English have always had more faith in competitive examinations than any other people (except perhaps the Imperial Chinese): they have conducted these examinations with traditional justice: but they have often shown remarkable woodenness in deciding what the examinations should be like. That is, incidentally, true to this day. It was certainly true of the Mathematical Tripos in its glory. It was an examination in which the questions were usually of considerable mechanical difficulty—but unfortunately did not give any opportunity for the candidate to show mathematical imagination or insight or any quality that a creative mathematician needs. The top candidates (the Wranglers—a term which still survives, meaning a First Class) were arranged, on the basis of marks, in strict numerical order. Colleges had celebrations when one of their number became Senior Wrangler: the first two or three Wranglers were immediately elected Fellows.

It was all very English. It had only one disadvantage, as Hardy pointed out with his polemic clarity, as soon as he had become an eminent mathematician and was engaged, together with his tough ally Littlewood, in getting the system abolished: it had effectively ruined serious mathematics in England for a hundred years.

In his first term at Trinity, Hardy found himself caught in this system. He was to be trained as a racehorse, over a course of mathematical exercises which at nineteen he knew to be meaningless. He was sent to a famous coach, to whom most potential Senior Wranglers went.

This coach knew all the obstacles, all the tricks of the examiners, and was sublimely uninterested in the subject itself. At this point the young Einstein would have rebelled: he would either have left Cambridge or done no formal work for the next three years. But Hardy was born into the more intensely professional English climate (which has its merits as well as its demerits). After considering changing his subject to history, he had the sense to find a real mathematician to teach him. Hardy paid him a tribute in the *Apology*: "My eyes were first opened by Professor Love, who taught me for a few terms and gave me my first serious conception of analysis. But the great debt which I owe to him—he was, after all, primarily an applied mathematician—was his advice to read Jordan's famous *Cours d'Analyse*; and I shall never forget the astonishment with which I read that remarkable work, the first inspiration for so many mathematicians of my generation, and learned for the first time as I read it what mathematics really meant. From that time onwards I was in my way a real mathematician, with sound mathematical ambitions and a genuine passion for mathematics."

He was fourth Wrangler in 1898. This faintly irritated him, he used to confess. He was enough of a natural competitor to feel that, though the race was ridiculous, he ought to have won it. In 1900 he took Part II of the Tripos, a more respect-worthy examination, and got his right place and his Fellowship.

From that time on, his life was in essence settled. He knew his purpose, which was to bring rigor into English mathematical analysis. He did not deviate from the researches which he called "the one great permanent happiness of my life." There were no anxieties about what he should do. Neither he nor anyone else doubted his great talent. He was elected to the Royal Society at thirty-three.

In many senses, then, he was unusually lucky. He did not have to think about his career. From the time he was twenty-three he had all the leisure that a man could want, and as much money as he needed. A bachelor don in Trinity in the 1900's was comfortably off. Hardy was sensible about money, spent it when he felt impelled (sometimes for singular purposes, such as fifty-mile taxi-rides), and otherwise was not at all unworldly about investments. He played his games and indulged in his eccentricities. He was living in some of the best intellectual company in the world—G. E. Moore, Whitehead, Bertrand Russell, Trevelyan, the high Trinity society which was shortly to find its artistic complement in Bloomsbury. (Hardy himself had links with Bloomsbury, both of personal friendship and of sympathy.) In a brilliant circle, he was one of the most brilliant young men—and, in a quiet way, one of the most irrepressible.

I will anticipate now what I shall say later. His life remained the life of a brilliant young man until he was old: so did his spirit: his games, his interests, kept the lightness of a young don's. And, like many of those who keep a young man's interests into their sixties, his last years were the darker for it.

Much of his life, though, he was happier than most of us. He had a great many friends, of surprisingly different kinds. These friends had to pass some of his private tests: they needed to possess a quality which he called "spin" (this is a cricket term, and untranslatable: it implies a certain obliquity or irony of approach: of recent public figures, Macmillan and Kennedy would get high marks for spin, Churchill and Eisenhower not). But he was tolerant, loyal, extremely high-spirited, and in an undemonstrative way fond of his friends. I once was compelled to go and see him in the morning, which was always his set time for mathematical work. He was sitting at his desk, writing in his beautiful calligraphy. I murmured some commonplace politeness about hoping that I wasn't disturbing him. He suddenly dissolved into his mischievous grin. "As you ought to be able to notice, the answer to that is that you are. Still, I'm usually glad to see you." In the sixteen years we knew each other, he didn't say anything more demonstrative than that: except on his death-bed, when he told me that he looked forward to my visits.

I think my experience was shared by most of his close friends. But he had, scattered through his life, two or three other relationships, different in kind. These were intense affections, absorbing, non-physical but exalted. The one I knew about was for a young man whose nature was as spiritually delicate as his own. I believe, though I only picked this up from chance remarks, that the same was true of the others. To many people of my generation, such relationships would seem either unsatisfactory or impossible. They were neither the one nor the other; and, unless one takes them for granted, one doesn't begin to understand the temperament of men like Hardy (they are rare, but not as rare as white rhinoceroses), nor the Cambridge society of his time. He didn't get the satisfactions that most of us can't help finding: but he knew himself unusually well, and that didn't make him unhappy. His inner life was his own, and very rich. The sadness came at the end. Apart from his devoted sister, he was left with no one close to him.

With sardonic stoicism he says in the *Apology*—which for all its high spirits is a book of desperate sadness—that when a creative man has lost the power or desire to create, "It is a pity but in that case he does not matter a great deal anyway, and it would be silly to bother about him." That is how he treated his personal life outside mathematics. Mathematics was his justification. It was easy to forget this, in the sparkle of his company: just as it was easy in the presence of Einstein's moral passion to forget that to himself his justification was his search for the physical laws. Neither of those two ever forgot it. This was the core of their lives, from young manhood to death.

Hardy, unlike Einstein, did not make a quick start. His early papers, between 1900 and 1911, were good enough to get him into the Royal Society and win him an international reputation: but he did not regard them as important. Again, this wasn't false modesty: it was the judgment of a master who knew to an inch which of his work had value and which hadn't.

In 1911 he began a collaboration with Littlewood which lasted thirty-five years. In 1913 he discovered Ramanujan and began another collaboration. All his major work was done in these two partnerships, most of it in the one with Littlewood, the most famous collaboration in the history of mathematics. There has been nothing like it in any science, or, so far as I know, in any other field of creative activity. Together they produced nearly a hundred papers, a good many of them "in the Bradman class." Mathematicians not intimate with Hardy in his later years, nor with cricket, keep repeating that his highest term of praise was "in the Hobbs class." It wasn't: very reluctantly, because Hobbs was one of his pets, he had to alter the order of merit. I once had a postcard from him, probably in 1938, saying: "Bradman is a whole class above any batsman who has ever lived: if Archimedes, Newton and Gauss remain in the Hobbs class, I have to admit the possibility of a class above them, which I find difficult to imagine. They had better be moved from now on into the Bradman class."

The Hardy-Littlewood researches dominated English pure mathematics, and much of world pure mathematics, for a generation. It is too early to say, so mathematicians tell me, to what extent they altered the course of mathematical analysis: nor how influential their work will appear in a hundred years. Of its enduring value there is no question.

Theirs was, as I have said, the greatest of all collaborations. But no one knows how they did it: unless Littlewood tells us, no one will ever know. I have already given Hardy's judgment that Littlewood was the more powerful mathematician of the two: Hardy once wrote that he knew of "no one else who could command such a combination of insight, technique and power." Littlewood was and is a more normal man than Hardy, just as interesting and probably more complex. He never had Hardy's taste for a kind of refined intellectual flamboyance, and so was less in the center of the academic scene. This led to jokes

G. H. Hardy ✻ 37

from European mathematicians, such as that Hardy had invented him so as to take the blame in case there turned out anything wrong with one of their theorems. In fact, he is a man of at least as obstinate an individuality as Hardy himself.

At first glance, neither of them would have seemed the easiest of partners. It is hard to imagine either of them suggesting the collaboration in the first place. Yet one of them must have done. No one has any evidence how they set about it. Through their most productive period, they were not at the same university. Harald Bohr (brother of Niels Bohr, and himself a fine mathematician) is reported as saying that one of their principles was this: if one wrote a letter to the other, the recipient was under no obligation to reply to it, or even to read it.

I can't contribute anything. Hardy talked to me, over a period of many years, on almost every conceivable subject, except the collaboration. He said, of course, that it had been the major fortune of his creative career: he spoke of Littlewood in the terms I have given: but he never gave a hint of their procedures. I didn't know enough mathematics to understand their papers, but I picked up some of their language. If he had let slip anything about their methods, I don't think I should have missed it. I am fairly certain that the secrecy—quite uncharacteristic of him in matters which to most would seem more intimate—was deliberate.

About his discovery of Ramanujan, he showed no secrecy at all. It was, he wrote, the one romantic incident in his life: anyway, it is an admirable story, and one which showers credit on nearly everyone (with two exceptions) in it. One morning early in 1913, he found, among the letters on his breakfast table, a large, untidy envelope decorated with Indian stamps. When he opened it, he found sheets of paper by no means fresh, on which, in a non-English holograph, were line after line of symbols. Hardy glanced at them without enthusiasm. He was by this time, at the age of thirty-six, a world-famous mathematician: and world-famous mathematicians, he had already discovered, are unusually exposed to cranks. He was accustomed to receiving manuscripts from strangers, proving the prophetic wisdom of the Great Pyramid, the revelations of the Elders of Zion, or the cryptograms that Bacon had inserted in the plays of the so-called Shakespeare.

So Hardy felt, more than anything, bored. He glanced at the letter, written in halting English, signed by an unknown Indian, asking him to give an opinion of these mathematical discoveries. The script appeared to consist of theorems, most of them wild or fantastic looking, one or two already well known, laid out as though they were original. There were no proofs of any kind. Hardy was not only bored, but irritated. It seemed like a curious kind of fraud. He put the manuscript aside, and went on with his day's routine. Since that routine did not vary throughout his life, it is possible to reconstruct it. First he read *The Times* over his breakfast. This happened in January, and if there were any Australian cricket scores, he would start with them, studied with clarity and intense attention.

Maynard Keynes, who began his career as a mathematician and who was a friend of Hardy's, once scolded him: if he had read the stock exchange quotations half an hour each day with the same concentration he brought to the cricket scores, he could not have helped becoming a rich man.

Then, from about nine to one, unless he was giving a lecture, he worked at his own mathematics. Four hours' creative work a day is about the limit for a mathematician, he used to say. Lunch, a light meal, in hall. After lunch he loped off for a game of real tennis in the university court. (If it had been summer, he would have walked down to Fenner's to watch cricket.) In the late afternoon, a stroll back to his rooms. That particular day, though, while the timetable wasn't altered, internally things were not going according to plan. At the back of his mind, getting in the way of his complete pleasure in his game, the Indian manuscript nagged away. Wild theorems. Theorems such as he had never seen before, nor imagined. A fraud of genius? A question was forming itself in his mind. As it was Hardy's mind, the question was forming itself with epigrammatic clarity: is a fraud of genius more probable than an unknown mathematician of genius? Clearly the answer was no. Back in his rooms in Trinity, he had another look at the script. He sent word to Littlewood (probably by messenger, certainly not by telephone, for which, like all mechanical contrivances including fountain pens, he had a deep distrust) that they must have a discussion after hall.

When the meal was over, there may have been a slight delay. Hardy liked a glass of wine, but, despite the glorious vistas of "Alan St. Aubyn" which had fired his youthful imagination, he found he did not really enjoy lingering in the combination-room over port and walnuts. Littlewood, a good deal more *homme moyen sensuel,* did. So there may have been a delay. Anyway, by nine o'clock or so they were in one of Hardy's rooms, with the manuscript stretched out in front of them.

That is an occasion at which one would have liked to be present. Hardy with his combination of remorseless clarity and intellectual panache (he was very English, but in argument he showed the characteristics that Latin minds have often assumed to be their own): Littlewood, imaginative, powerful, humorous. Apparently it did not take them long. Before midnight they knew, and knew for certain. The writer of these manuscripts was a man of genius. That was as much as they could judge, that night. It was only later that Hardy decided that Ramanujan was, in terms of *natural* mathematical genius, in the class of Gauss and Euler: but that he could not expect, because of the defects of his education, and because he had come on the scene too late in the line of mathematical history, to make a contribution on the same scale.

It all sounds easy, the kind of judgment great mathematicians should have been able to make. But I mentioned that there were two persons who do not come out of the story with credit. Out of chivalry Hardy concealed this in all that he said or wrote about Ramanujan. The two people concerned have now been dead, however, for many years, and it is time to tell the truth. It is simple. Hardy was not the first eminent mathematician to be sent the Ramanujan manuscripts. There had been two before him, both English, both of the highest professional standard. They had each returned the manuscripts without comment. I don't think history relates what they said, if anything, when Ramanujan became famous. Anyone who has been sent unsolicited material will have a sneaking sympathy with them.

Anyway, the following day Hardy went into action. Ramanujan must be brought to England, Hardy decided. Money was not a major problem. Trinity has usually been good at supporting unorthodox talent (the college did the same for Kapitsa a few years later). Once Hardy was determined, no human agency could have stopped Ramanujan, but they needed a certain amount of help from a superhuman one.

Ramanujan turned out to be a poor clerk in Madras, living with his wife on twenty pounds a year. But he was also a Brahmin, unusually strict about his religious observances, with a mother who was even stricter. It seemed impossible that he could break the proscriptions and cross the water. Fortunately his mother had the highest respect for the goddess of Namakkal. One morning Ramanujan's mother made a startling announcement. She had had a dream on the previous night in which she saw her son seated in a big hall among a group of Europeans, and the goddess of Namakkal had commanded her not to stand in the way of her son fulfilling his life's purpose. This, say Ramanujan's Indian biographers, was a very agreeable surprise to all concerned.

In 1914 Ramanujan arrived in England. So far as Hardy could detect (though in this respect I should not trust his insight far) Ramanujan, despite the difficulties of breaking the caste proscriptions, did not believe much in theological doctrine, except for a vague pantheistic benevolence, any more than Hardy did himself. But he did certainly believe in ritual. When Trinity put him up in college—within four years he became a Fellow—there was no "Alan St. Aubyn" apolausticity for him at all. Hardy used to find him ritually changed into his pajamas, cooking vegetables rather miserably in a frying pan in his own room.

Their association was a strangely touching one. Hardy did not forget that he was in the presence of genius: but genius that was, even in mathematics, almost untrained. Ramanujan had not been able to enter Madras University because he could not matriculate in English. According to Hardy's report, he was always amiable and good-natured, but no doubt he sometimes found Hardy's conversation outside mathematics more than a little baffling. He seems to have listened with a patient smile on his good, friendly, homely face. Even inside mathematics they had to come to terms with the difference in their education. Ramanujan was self-taught: he knew nothing of the modern rigor: in a sense he didn't know what a proof was. In an uncharacteristically sloppy moment, Hardy once wrote that if he had been better educated, he would have been less Ramanujan. Coming back to his ironic senses, Hardy later corrected himself and said that the statement was nonsense. If Ramanujan had been better educated, he would have been even more wonderful than he was. In fact, Hardy was obliged to teach him some formal mathematics, as though Ramanujan had been a scholarship candidate at Winchester. Hardy said that this was the most singular experience of his life: what did modern mathematics look like to someone who had the deepest insight, but who had literally never heard of most of it?

Anyway, they produced together five papers of the highest class, in which Hardy showed supreme originality of his own (more is known of the details of this collaboration than of the Hardy-Littlewood one). Generosity and imagination were, for once, rewarded in full.

This is a story of human virtue. Once people had started behaving well, they went on behaving better. It is good to remember that England gave Ramanujan such honors as were possible. The Royal Society elected him a Fellow at the age of thirty (which, even for a mathematician, is very young). Trinity also elected him a Fellow in the same year. He was the first Indian to be given either of these distinctions. He was amiably grateful. But he soon became ill. It was difficult, in war-time, to move him to a kinder climate.

Hardy used to visit him, as he lay dying in hospital at Putney. It was on one of those visits that there happened the incident of the taxi-cab number. Hardy had gone out to Putney by taxi, as usual his chosen method of conveyance. He went into the room where Ramanujan was lying. Hardy, always inept about introducing a conversation, said, probably without a greeting, and certainly as his first remark: "The number of my taxi-cab was 1729. It seemed to me rather a dull number." To which Ramanujan replied: "No, Hardy! No, Hardy! It is a very interesting number. It is the smallest number expressible as the sum of two cubes in two different ways."

That is the exchange as Hardy recorded it. It must be

substantially accurate. He was the most honest of men; and further, no one could possibly have invented it.

Ramanujan died of tuberculosis, back in Madras, two years after the war. As Hardy wrote in the *Apology*, in his roll-call of mathematicians: "Galois died at twenty-one, Abel at twenty-seven, Ramanujan at thirty-three, Riemann at forty. . . . I do not know an instance of a major mathematical advance initiated by a man past fifty."

If it had not been for the Ramanujan collaboration, the 1914–18 war would have been darker for Hardy than it was. But it was dark enough. It left a wound which reopened in the second war. He was a man of radical opinions all his life. His radicalism, though, was tinged with the turn-of-the-century enlightenment. To people of my generation, it sometimes seemed to breathe a lighter, more innocent air than the one we knew.

Like many of his Edwardian intellectual friends, he had a strong feeling for Germany. Germany had, after all, been the great educating force of the nineteenth century. To Eastern Europe, to Russia, to the United States, it was the German universities which had taught the meaning of research. Hardy hadn't much use for German philosophy or German literature: his tastes were too classical for that. But in most respects the German culture, including its social welfare, appeared to him higher than his own.

Unlike Einstein, who had a much more rugged sense of political existence, Hardy did not know much of Wilhelmine Germany at first hand. And, though he was the least vain of people, he would have been less than human if he had not enjoyed being more appreciated in Germany than in his own country. There is a pleasant anecdote, dating from this period, in which Hilbert, one of the greatest of German mathematicians, heard that Hardy lived in a not specially agreeable set of rooms in Trinity (actually in Whewell's Court). Hilbert promptly wrote in measured terms to the Master, pointing out that Hardy was the best mathematician, not only in Trinity but in England, and should therefore have the best rooms.

So Hardy, like Russell and many of the high Cambridge intelligentsia, did not believe that the war should have been fought. Further, with his ingrained distrust of English politicians, he thought the balance of wrong was on the English side. He could not find a satisfactory basis for conscientious objection; his intellectual rigor was too strong for that. In fact, he volunteered for service under the Derby scheme, and was rejected on medical grounds. But he felt increasingly isolated in Trinity, much of which was vociferously bellicose.

Russell was dismissed from his lectureship, in circumstances of overheated complexity (Hardy was to write the only detailed account of the case a quarter of a century later, in order to comfort himself in another war). Hardy's close friends were away at the war. Littlewood was doing ballistics as a Second Lieutenant in the Royal Artillery. Owing to his cheerful indifference he had the distinction of remaining a Second Lieutenant through the four years of war. Their collaboration was interfered with, though not entirely stopped. It was the work of Ramanujan which was Hardy's solace during the bitter college quarrels.

I sometimes thought he was, for once, less than fair to his colleagues. Some were pretty crazed, as men are in war-time. But some were long-suffering and tried to keep social manners going. After all, it was a triumph of academic uprightness that they should have elected his protégé Ramanujan, at a time when Hardy was only just on speaking terms with some of the electors, and not at all with others.

Still, he was harshly unhappy. As soon as he could, he left Cambridge. He was offered a chair at Oxford in 1919: and immediately walked into the happiest time of his life. He had already done great work with Ramanujan and Littlewood, but now the collaboration with Littlewood rose to its full power. Hardy was, in Newton's phrase, "in the prime of his life for invention," and this came in his early forties, unusually late for a mathematician.

Coming so late, this creative surge gave him the feeling, more important to him than to most men, of timeless youth. He was living the young man's life which was first nature to him. He played more real tennis, and got steadily better at it (real tennis was an expensive game and took a largish slice out of a professorial income). He made a good many visits to American universities, and loved the country. He was one of the few Englishmen of his time who was fond, to an extent approximately equal, of the United States and the Soviet Union. He was certainly the only Englishman of his or any other time who wrote a serious suggestion to the Baseball Commissioners, proposing a technical emendation to one of the rules. The twen-

ties, for him and for most liberals of his generation, was a
false dawn. He thought the misery of the war was swept
away into the past.

He was at home in New College as he had never been
in Cambridge. The warm domestic conversational Oxford
climate was good for him. It was there, in a college at that
time small and intimate, that he perfected his own style of
conversation. There was company eager to listen to him
after hall. They could take his eccentricities. He was not
only a great and good man, they realized, but an entertain-
ing one. If he wanted to play conversational games, or real
(though bizarre) games on the cricket field, they were
ready to act as foils. In a casual and human fashion, they
made a fuss of him. He had been admired and esteemed
before, but not made a fuss of in that fashion.

No one seemed to care—it was a gossipy college joke
—that he had a large photograph of Lenin in his rooms.
Hardy's radicalism was somewhat unorganized, but it was
real. He had been born, as I have explained, into a professional family: almost all his life was spent among the
haute bourgeoisie: but in fact he behaved much more like
an aristocrat, or more exactly like one of the more romantic
projections of an aristocrat. Some of this attitude, perhaps,
he had picked up from his friend Bertrand Russell. But
most of it was innate. Underneath his shyness, he just
didn't give a damn.

He got on easily, without any patronage, with the
poor, the unlucky and diffident, those who were handi-
capped by race (it was a symbolic stroke of fate that he
discovered Ramanujan). He preferred them to the people
whom he called "the large bottomed": the description was

more psychological than physiological, though there was a famous nineteenth century Trinity aphorism by Adam Sedgwick: "No one ever made a success in this world without a large bottom." To Hardy the large bottomed were the confident, booming, imperialist bourgeois English. The designation included most bishops, headmasters, judges, and all politicians, with the single exception of Lloyd George.

Just to show his allegiances, he accepted one public office. For two years (1924–26) he was President of the Association of Scientific Workers. He said sarcastically that he was an odd choice, being "the most unpractical member of the most unpractical profession in the world." But in important things he was not so unpractical. He was deliberately standing up to be counted. When, much later, I came to work with Frank Cousins, it gave me a certain quiet pleasure to reflect that I had exactly two friends who had held office in the Trade Union movement, him and G. H. Hardy.

That late, not quite Indian, summer in Oxford in the twenties, was so happy that people wondered that he ever returned to Cambridge. Which he did in 1931. I think there were two reasons. First and most decisive, he was a great professional. Cambridge was still the center of English mathematics, and the senior mathematical chair there was the correct place for a professional. Second, and rather oddly, he was thinking about his old age. Oxford colleges, in many ways so human and warm, are ruthless with the old: if he remained at New College he would be turned out of his rooms as soon as he retired, at the age of sixty-five, from his professorship. Whereas, if he returned to Trinity, he could stay in college until he died. That is in effect what he managed to do.

When he came back to Cambridge—which was the time that I began to know him—he was in the afterglow of his great period. He was still happy. He was still creative, not so much as in the twenties, but enough to make him feel that the power was still there. He was as spirited as he had been at New College. So we had the luck to see him very nearly at his best.

In the winters, after we had become friendly, we gave each other dinner in our respective colleges once a fortnight. In the summer, it was taken for granted that we should meet at the cricket ground. Except on special occasions he still did mathematics in the morning, and did not arrive at Fenner's until after lunch. He used to walk round the cinderpath with a long, loping, clumping-footed stride (he was a slight, spare man, physically active even in his late fifties, still playing real tennis), head down, hair, tie, sweaters, papers all flowing, a figure that caught everyone's eyes. "There goes a Greek poet, I'll be bound," once said some cheerful farmer as Hardy passed the score-board. He made for his favorite place, opposite the pavilion, where he could catch each ray of sun—he was obsessively heliotropic. In order to deceive the sun into shining, he brought with him, even on a fine May afternoon, what he called his "anti-God battery." This consisted of three or four sweaters, an umbrella belonging to his sister, and a large envelope containing mathematical manuscripts, such as a Ph.D. dissertation, a paper which he was refereeing for the Royal Society, or some Tripos answers. He would explain to an acquaintance that God, believing that Hardy expected the weather to change and give him a chance to work, counter-suggestibly arranged that the sky should remain cloudless.

There he sat. To complete his pleasure in a long afternoon watching cricket, he liked the sun to be shining and a companion to join in the fun. Technique, tactics, formal beauty—those were the deepest attractions of the game for him. I won't try to explain them: they are in-communicable unless one knows the language: just as some of Hardy's classical aphorisms are inexplicable unless one knows either the language of cricket or of the theory of numbers, and preferably both. Fortunately for a good many of our friends, he also had a relish for the human comedy.

He would have been the first to disclaim that he had any special psychological insight. But he was the most in-telligent of men, he had lived with his eyes open and read a lot, and he had obtained a good generalized sense of human nature—robust, indulgent, satirical, and utterly free from moral vanity. He was spiritually candid as few men are (I doubt if anyone could be more candid), and he had a mocking horror of pretentiousness, self-righteous indignation, and the whole stately pantechnicon of the hypocritical virtues. Now cricket, the most beautiful of games, is also the most hypocritical. It is supposed to be the ultimate expression of the team spirit. One ought to prefer to make 0 and see one's side win, than make 100 and see it lose (one very great player, like Hardy a man of innocent candor, once remarked mildly that he never managed to feel so). This particular ethos inspired Hardy's sense of the ridiculous. In reply he used to expound a counter-balancing series of maxims. Examples:

Cricket is the only game where you are playing against eleven of the other side and ten of your own.

If you are nervous when you go in first, nothing restores your confidence so much as seeing the other man get out.

If his listeners were lucky, they would hear other remarks, not relevant to cricket, as sharp-edged in conversation as in his writing. In the *Apology* there are some typical specimens: here are a few more.

It is never worth a first class man's time to express a majority opinion. By definition, there are plenty of others to do that.

When I was an undergraduate one might, if one were sufficiently unorthodox, suggest that Tolstoi came within touching distance of George Meredith as a novelist: but, of course, no one else possibly could. [This was said about the intoxications of fashion: it is worth remembering that he had lived in one of the most brilliant of all Cambridge generations.]

For any serious purpose, intelligence is a very minor gift.

Young men ought to be conceited: but they oughtn't to be imbecile. [Said after someone had tried to persuade him that *Finnegan's Wake* was the final literary masterpiece.]

Sometimes one has to say difficult things, but one ought to say them as simply as one knows how.

Occasionally, as he watched cricket, his ball-by-ball interest flagged. Then he demanded that we should pick teams: teams of humbugs, club-men, bogus poets, bores, teams whose names began with HA (numbers one and two Hadrian and Hannibal), SN, all-time teams of Trinity, Christ's, and so on. In these exercises I was at a disadvantage: let anyone try to produce a team of world figures whose names start with SN. The Trinity team is overwhelmingly strong (Clerk Maxwell, Byron, Thackeray, Tennyson aren't certain of places): while Christ's, beginning strongly with Milton and Darwin, has nothing much to show from number 3 down.

Or he had another favorite entertainment. "Mark that man we met last night," he said, and someone had to be marked out of 100 in each of the categories Hardy had long since invented and defined. STARK, BLEAK ("a stark man is not necessarily bleak: but all bleak men without exception want to be considered stark"), DIM, OLD BRANDY, SPIN, and some others. STARK, BLEAK and DIM are self-explanatory (the Duke of Wellington would get a flat 100 for STARK and BLEAK, and 0 for DIM). OLD BRANDY was derived from a mythical character who said that he never drank anything but old brandy. Hence, by extrapolation, OLD BRANDY came to mean a taste that was eccentric, esoteric, but just within the bounds of reason. As a character (and in Hardy's view, though not mine, as a writer also) Proust got high marks for OLD BRANDY: so did F. A. Lindemann (later Lord Cherwell).

The summer days passed. After one of the short Cambridge seasons, there was the university match. Arranging to meet him in London was not always simple, for he had a morbid suspicion of mechanical gadgets (he never used a watch), in particular of the telephone. In his rooms in Trinity or his flat in St. George's Square, he used to say, in a disapproving and slightly sinister tone: "If you *fancy*

G. H. Hardy 53

yourself at the telephone, there is one in the next room."
Once in an emergency he had to ring me up: angrily his
voice came at me: "I shan't hear a word you say, so when
I'm finished I shall immediately put the receiver down.
It's important you should come round between nine and
ten tonight." Clonk.

Yet, punctually, he arrived at the university match.
There he was at his most sparkling, year after year. Surrounded by friends, men and women, he was quite re-
leased from shyness. He was the center of all our attention, which he didn't dislike. Sometimes one could hear
the party's laughter from a quarter of the way round the
ground.

In those last of his happy years, everything he did
was light with grace, order, a sense of style. Cricket is a
game of grace and order, which is why he found formal
beauty in it. His mathematics, so I am told, had those
same aesthetic qualities, right up to his last creative work.
I have given the impression, I fancy, that in private he
was a conversational performer. To an extent, that was
true: but he was also, on what he would have called non-
trivial occasions (meaning occasions important to either
participant), a serious and concentrated listener. Of the
others about whom I am now writing and whom I knew
at the same period, Wells was, on the whole, a worse listener than one expected: Rutherford distinctly better:
Lloyd George one of the best listeners of all time. Hardy
didn't suck impressions and knowledge out of others'
words, as Lloyd George did, but his mind was at one's dis-
posal. When, years before I wrote it, he heard of the concept of *The Masters,* he cross-examined me, so that I did

most of the talking. He produced some good ideas. I wish
he had been able to read the book, which I think that he
might have liked. Anyway, in that hope I dedicated it to
his memory.

In the note at the end of the *Apology* he refers to
other discussions. One of these was long-drawn-out, and
sometimes, on both sides, angry. On the Second World War
we each had passionate but, as I shall have to say a little
later, different opinions. I didn't shift his by one inch.
Nevertheless, though we were separated by a gulf of emotion, on the plane of reason he recognized what I was saying. That was true in any argument I had with him.

Through the thirties he lived his own version of a
young man's life. Then suddenly it broke. In 1939 he had
a coronary thrombosis. He recovered, but real tennis,
squash, the physical activities he loved, were over for
good. The war darkened him still further, just as the first
war had. To him they were connected pieces of lunacy,
we were all at fault, he couldn't identify himself with the
war—once it was clear the country would survive—any
more than he had done in 1914. One of his closest friends
died tragically. And—I think there is no doubt these
griefs were inter-connected—his creative powers as a
mathematician at last, in his sixties, left him.

That is why *A Mathematician's Apology* is, if read
with the textual attention it deserves, a book of such
haunting sadness. Yes, it is witty and sharp with intellectual high spirits: yes, the crystalline clarity and candor
are still there: yes, it is the testament of a creative artist.
But it is also, in an understated stoical fashion, a passionate lament for creative powers that used to be and that

G. H. Hardy ❈ 55

will never come again. I know nothing like it in the language: partly because most people with the literary gift to express such a lament don't come to feel it: it is very rare for a writer to realize, with the finality of truth, that he is absolutely finished.

Seeing him in those years, I couldn't help thinking of the price he was paying for his young man's life. It was like seeing a great athlete, for years in the pride of his youth and skill, so much younger and more joyful than the rest of us, suddenly have to accept that the gift has gone. It is common to meet great athletes who have gone, as they call it, over the hill: fairly quickly the feet get heavier (often the eyes last longer), the strokes won't come off, Wimbledon is a place to be dreaded, the crowds go to watch someone else. That is the point at which a good many athletes take to drink. Hardy didn't take to drink: but he took to something like despair. He recovered enough physically to have ten minutes batting at the nets, or to play his pleasing elaboration (with a complicated set of bisques) of Trinity bowls. But it was often hard to rouse his interest—three or four years before his interest in everything was so sparkling as sometimes to tire us all out. "No one should ever be bored," had been one of his axioms. "One can be horrified, or disgusted, but one can't be bored." Yet now he was often just that, plain bored.

It was for that reason that some of his friends, including me, encouraged him to write the story of Bertrand Russell and Trinity in the 1914–18 war. People who didn't know how depressed Hardy was thought the whole episode was now long over and ought not to be resurrected. The truth was, it enlivened him to have any kind of purpose. The book was privately circulated. It has never been obtainable by the public, which is a pity, for it is a small-scale addition to academic history.

I used such persuasion as I had to get him to write another book, which he had in happier days promised me to do. It was to be called *A Day at the Oval* and was to consist of himself watching cricket for a whole day, spreading himself in disquisitions on the game, human nature, his reminiscences, life in general. It would have been an eccentric minor classic: but it was never written.

I wasn't much help to him in those last years. I was deeply involved in war-time Whitehall, I was preoccupied and often tired, it was an effort to get to Cambridge. But I ought to have made the effort more often than I did. I have to admit, with remorse, that there was, not exactly a chill, but a gap in sympathy between us. He lent me his flat in Pimlico—a dark and seedy flat with the St. George's Square gardens outside and what he called an "old brandy" attractiveness—for the whole of the war. But he didn't like me being so totally committed. People he approved of oughtn't to give themselves whole-heartedly to military functions. He never asked me about my work. He didn't want to talk about the war. While I, for my part, was impatient and didn't show anything like enough consideration. After all, I thought, I wasn't doing this job for fun: as I had to do it, I might as well extract the maximum interest. But that is no excuse.

At the end of the war I did not return to Cambridge. I visited him several times in 1946. His depression had not lifted, he was physically failing, short of breath after a few yards' walk. The long, cheerful stroll across Parker's Piece, after the close of play, was gone for ever: I had to take him home to Trinity in a taxi. He was glad that I had gone back to writing books: the creative life was the only one for a serious man. As for himself, he wished that he could live the creative life again, no better than it had been before: his own life was over.

I am not quoting his exact words. This was so unlike him that I wanted to forget, and I tried, by a kind of irony, to smear over what had just been said. So that I have never remembered precisely. I attempted to dismiss it to myself as a rhetorical flourish.

In the early summer of 1947 I was sitting at breakfast when the telephone rang. It was Hardy's sister: he was seriously ill, would I come up to Cambridge at once, would I call at Trinity first? At the time I didn't grasp the meaning of the second request. But I obeyed it, and in the porter's lodge at Trinity that morning found a note from her: I was to go to Donald Robertson's rooms, he would be waiting for me.

Donald Robertson was the Professor of Greek, and an intimate friend of Hardy's: he was another member of the same high, liberal, graceful Edwardian Cambridge. Incidentally, he was one of the few people who called Hardy by his Christian name. He greeted me quietly. Outside the windows of his room it was a calm and sunny morning. He said:

"You ought to know that Harold has tried to kill himself."

Yes, he was out of danger: he was for the time being all right, if that was the phrase to use. But Donald was, in a less pointed fashion, as direct as Hardy himself. It was a pity the attempt had failed. Hardy's health had got worse: he could not in any case live long: even walking from his rooms to hall had become a strain. He had made a completely deliberate choice. Life on those terms he would not endure: there was nothing in it. He had collected enough barbiturates: he had tried to do a thorough job, and had taken too many.

I was fond of Donald Robertson, but I had met him only at parties and at Trinity high table. This was the first occasion on which we had talked intimately. He said, with gentle firmness, that I ought to come up to see Hardy as often as I could: it would be hard to take, but it was an obligation: probably it would not be for long. We were both wretched. I said goodbye, and never saw him again.

In the Evelyn nursing home, Hardy was lying in bed. As a touch of farce, he had a black eye. Vomiting from the drugs, he had hit his head on the lavatory basin. He was self-mocking. He had made a mess of it. Had anyone ever made a bigger mess? I had to enter into the sarcastic game. I had never felt less like sarcasm, but I had to play. I talked about other distinguished failures at bringing off suicide. What about German generals in the last war? Beck, Stülpnagel, they had been remarkably incompetent at it. It was bizarre to hear myself saying these things. Curiously enough, it seemed to cheer him up.

After that, I went to Cambridge at least once a week. I dreaded each visit, but early on he said that he looked forward to seeing me. He talked a little, nearly every time I saw him, about death. He wanted it: he didn't fear it: what was there to fear in nothingness? His hard intellectual stoicism had come back. He would not try to kill himself again. He wasn't good at it. He was prepared to wait. With an inconsistency which might have pained him—for he, like most of his circle, believed in the rational to an extent that I thought irrational—he showed an intense hypochondriac curiosity about his own symptoms. Constantly he was studying the oedema of his ankles: was it greater or less that day?

Mostly, though—about fifty-five minutes in each hour I was with him—I had to talk cricket. It was his only solace. I had to pretend a devotion to the game which I no longer felt, which in fact had been luke-warm in the thirties except for the pleasure of his company. Now I had to study the cricket scores as intently as when I was a schoolboy. He couldn't read for himself, but he would have known if I was bluffing. Sometimes, for a few minutes, his old vivacity would light up. But if I couldn't think of another question or piece of news, he would lie there, in the kind of dark loneliness that comes to some people before they die.

Once or twice I tried to rouse him. Wouldn't it be worth while, even if it was a risk, to go and see one more cricket match together? I was now better off than I used to be, I said. I was prepared to stand him a taxi, his old familiar means of transport, to any cricket ground he liked to name. At that he brightened. He said that I might have a dead man on my hands. I replied that I was ready to cope. I thought that he might come: he knew, I knew, that his death could only be a matter of months: I wanted to see him have one afternoon of something like gaiety. The next time I visited him he shook his head in something like anger. No, he couldn't even try: there was no point in trying.

It was hard enough for me to have to talk cricket. It was harder for his sister, a charming, intelligent woman who had never married and who had spent much of her life looking after him. With a humorous skill not unlike his own old form, she collected every scrap of cricket news she could find, though she had never learned anything about the game.

Once or twice the sarcastic love of the human comedy came bursting out. Two or three weeks before his death, he heard from the Royal Society that he was to be given their highest honor, the Copley Medal. He gave his Mephistophelian grin, the first time I had seen it in full splendor in all those months. "Now I know that I must be pretty near the end. When people hurry up to give you honorific things there is exactly one conclusion to be drawn."

After I heard that, I think I visited him twice. The last time was four or five days before he died. There was an Indian test team playing in Australia, and we talked about them.

It was in that same week that he told his sister: "If I knew that I was going to die today, I think I should still want to hear the cricket scores."

He managed something very similar. Each evening that week before she left him, she read a chapter from a history of Cambridge University cricket. One such chapter contained the last words he heard, for he died suddenly, in the early morning.

G. H. Hardy　61

H. G. WELLS

I suppose that, living in Cambridge in the thirties, I was bound to run into Rutherford and Hardy some time or other. The university was more intimate then than now; though, now I come to think of it, I never exchanged a word with G. E. Moore or A. E. Housman. Perhaps it was also statistically probable that, beginning my literary career in that period, I should find myself meeting Wells. This duly happened: but the circumstances were a little odd.

In September 1934 I published *The Search*. It had a good reception. Publishers were bidding for me: one was trying to bring off an arrangement with an American firm by which they jointly guaranteed me an income for three years, so as to extricate me from Cambridge and send me off to write by the Mediterranean. In those days, for some esoteric reason, it was considered almost impossible to write except on the shores of the Mediterranean. All this was, of course, gratifying. Later that autumn a letter arrived on my breakfast table in college, addressed in an unknown handwriting, small and elegant.

It was signed H. G. Wells. He had read my book with the liveliest interest and sympathy, he said. Would I come up to London for lunch?

He was living at that time in a flat in Chiltern Court, next door to Baker Street Station. It was the same block of flats in which Arnold Bennett had died, four years before. With my usual obsessive punctuality, I arrived on time. I was shown into a small sitting room and told that Mr. Wells would join me. The minutes passed: I spent some of them staring down from the window into Baker Street: it was a horrible, dark November day, clouds hanging over the roof tops, a Holmes-and-Watson day, pouring with rain.

I had been asked for one o'clock, and it was after half-past. I was beginning to wonder what had gone wrong when the door opened. A small rotund form entered. "Ah, it's you," he said in that voice, at the same time hoarse and high-pitched, which no one ever exactly imitated. "They told me you were here."

I thought that was a bit unnecessary. So perhaps did he, for then he apologized for being late. As he did so, I could not help but realize that there was something on his mind. In his turn he walked over to the window, and stood with his back to me, looking at the rain.

"You're married, aren't you, Snow?" he said without turning round.

I replied that I was not.

"Anyway," he addressed the dismal street, "I could see from your book that you knew some things."

He was extremely glum. Why had he not a wife to look after him? Why had neither of us wives to look after us? Why, in particular, would someone called Moura not marry him?

This I found a very difficult question, since I had met him only for ten minutes and had never heard of Moura. I tried to cheer him up, though for me the conversation was scraping uncomfortably near the bone: I had recently lost someone whom I had much wanted to marry.

Why were we unluckier than other men, Wells demanded. It was impossible to understand Moura. What reasons could I suggest for her behavior? It was a good deal later before we sat down at last to lunch.

Lunch did not relieve the gloom. Wells was having a special diet and ate very little; I had a small lamb chop and some mashed potatoes. We had a bottle of wine, but Wells, who never drank much, took only half a glass. Occasionally he got off the subject of marriage. He was taking my novel as though it were straight, factual autobiography: nothing teaches writers, not even their own books. He assumed that I had had a disappointment in research, and so wanted to give it up. He didn't want me to. He had always wished that he had stayed a scientist. No doubt the scientific life had its dangers and its setbacks. No doubt it bruised one's ego as a literary life did. But it must be much more satisfying. And when one's work was done, what human honor could compare with the plain Mr.——, F.R.S.?

I remembered he had said something like that in one of his early books. Was it *The Food of the Gods?* No, he didn't want to talk about his books, he wasn't interested in them. He wanted to talk about marriage, Moura and the scientific life.

Then Moura herself entered. She had forgotten her latchkey, she said. She was then a woman in early middle-age, handsome, dashing, strong as Mother Russia. I didn't know anything of her heritage or history, I didn't even know her surname, but I gathered that she was Russian, probably an aristocrat, but on close terms with the post-revolutionary writers.

She sat down at the table and with gusto helped me finish the bottle of wine. She gave out well-being, she was cheerful. The temperature of the party began to rise. Wells was looking at her with love and irritation. She talked to him with down-to-earth affection. But Wells's irritation grew when she also talked to me. Wells disapproved. It was getting on for four, and he made it clear that it was time I went. "Come back and see us soon," said Moura. But I was not invited to Chiltern Court again, though I met him a good many times away from home.

I became fond of him, though I doubt whether I picked up very much that I could not have divined from his books. He was marvellously inventive, but that anyone can read for himself. In the scientific romances, such as *The First Men in the Moon* and *The War of the Worlds*, he invented more *literary* devices than most people do in their whole career. He was just as inventive when he applied his mind to games for children—or to war. Between 1900 and 1914 he made a whole set of practical prophecies, including the concepts of the tank and the military aircraft. That kind of foresight he shared with Churchill, and it was an aspect of Churchill, perhaps the only one, for which he had a genuine respect.

He was not born wise, but he had learned much wisdom. He was touchy and self-centered: self-centered rather than vain and self-assertive. If the universe behaved according to his pattern, he was ready and willing to be forgotten. More than any writer, he was careless about the personal memorial that he might leave. At the time I knew him, when his sales and reputation were both slipping and when he needed a devoted publisher to hold on until he was fashionable again (just as Macmillan did for Kipling), he took an impish pleasure in moving from firm to firm, screwing out advances which the books would never earn. He did not care. Most writers, even those who are convinced that at death they are going into oblivion, comfort themselves that their books may live for a time. One such—to whom the idea of personal immortality was ridiculous—told me that, if he could be assured for certain that his books would be read in a hundred years, everything, all the disappointments, all the bitternesses, would have been worth while.

Wells would have regarded that as the crassest sentimentality. He wouldn't know, so he didn't care. But, with a pleasing inconsistency, he cared a great deal when one of his books came out. I have seen a good many writers (and politicians and even loftier figures) upset by bad reviews: but I don't think I have seen anyone more immediately upset than Wells. He suspected conspiracies. He wanted to murder literary editors and critics. He didn't think his friends were protecting him. More likely, he hinted darkly, he hadn't any friends. Then in a few days it all blew over, and he seemed to have forgotten that the book had been published at all.

In many ways he was curiously impersonal. He could make fun of himself as the Little Man, which he often did. He could be tetchy. He could have moments of paranoia about reviews. He could discuss predicaments which were pressing on him, without concealment and without worrying much whether he had met his confidant before —as at that first lunch with me. Yet it takes an impersonal nature to be so indifferent to its audience. He could as easily have been brooding on paper.

Much of his life he had, of course, been doing precisely that. It is a pity that the autobiographical vividness of some of his best novels—*Tono-Bungay, Kipps, Love and Mr. Lewisham*—softened the impact of his real autobiography. As a rule, novelists should not write autobiographies, but his is a most unusual one. Reading it, one feels astonishment at the toughness of the human spirit. This wasn't a life many of us would have come through intact.

He was born at the extreme lower edge of the lower middle-class. In that he wasn't any different from Dickens or a lot of other English writers (the uncommon thing would be to be born in the real working class: this has not yet produced in England a writer of the highest caliber: I have not forgotten Lawrence, whose mother's influence made his childhood essentially petit bourgeois). No, the singularity about Wells's upbringing was that he lived in that special stratum of the lower middle-class which, in his time, were superior servants.

His father was an under-gardener; and not a successful under-gardener at that, because he lost his job and had to make some sort of living out of professional cricket (in those days another form of domestic service) and out of pathetic attempts to keep a shop. He made a very bad living, and for most of Wells's childhood he did not have enough to eat. His mother began life as a ladies' maid, and when the shop failed had to support the family through becoming housekeeper to a large country house. The best she could imagine or devise for her son (already demonstrably as clever as could be) was to bind him apprentice to a draper's at the age of thirteen. He escaped through a mixture of ineptitude and obduracy: and was promptly apprenticed to a pharmaceutical chemist. He escaped again: and was once more apprenticed to another draper's.

Later in his life he was funny in his imitations of how he tried to wait on customers. But it isn't easy to imagine an environment more shaming to a proud and gifted boy. Dickens's time in the blacking factory was bad enough, but Wells's was much longer drawn out. It took him all his childhood. He treated it more humorously than Dickens (compare *Kipps* with the fact that Dickens could not bear to treat his experience imaginatively): he was less wounded than Dickens: but he was wounded nevertheless.

It gave him some of his splendid, perky disrespect, as though from an early age he was determined not to give a touch of the cap to any human dignity, dignitary or position: but, I always fancied, it made him less realistic about politics, more prone to invent Utopias, in which splendid god-like figures went about arranging the world cleanly, making sure that there were no longer any wistful, imaginative little boys, sick, underfed and undersized, whistling to keep their courage up. Like Lloyd George, he was, in a deep sense, radical until he died. He made many fewer concessions than Lloyd George; he had less temptation to make them, not being a politician at all, much less a politician of genius. Neither of them forgot, nor perhaps forgave, their origins. Yet somehow they came from a social base which didn't make systematic political thinking easy. Neither of them was close to the industrial working class, though both had intimations of how in advanced societies it might develop. It is probably fair to say that no one in advanced societies has found systematic political thinking easy—unless it is the system of pure reaction—down to our own time.

Much later in his life, Wells had a meeting with Lenin which no one could call successful. Wells, though he thought that Lenin was a great man, described him as "the dreamer in the Kremlin." Lenin said, "What a little bourgeois!"

It was a pity. Wells had a knack of making phrases that pursued him for years. This was the most curiously inapposite of all of them. But he was always impatient about politics. He couldn't find his way through the inextricable dark muddle that has always been part of Russia: he couldn't realize that when Lenin talked of electrification, he was talking of something as practical (though as far from immediate hardware) as a blue print. Whereas Lenin, who had thought about politics every day of his adult life, could not believe that a man could be at the same time well intentioned, imaginative and unaware of what a revolutionary situation means.

Yet Wells was, right up to his death, better disposed to Russia than most Englishmen. He was a friend and rival of Gorky's: himself very brave, physically as well as mentally, he admired the Russians' guts. Somehow the Russians have responded to him. To this day, under the unfamiliar appellation of Herbert Wells, he is read in enormous editions in the Soviet Union.

Before that meeting with Lenin in 1920, when Wells was a world figure, he had had struggles much harsher than Dickens's or Shaw's or any other nineteenth century writer's. The wound of his childhood he soon, at least superficially, shrugged off: but he had to claw his way through illness that looked mortal, poverty that didn't help the illness, the effort just to survive; and, when he was just managing to survive, the strains produced by an abnormally ardent sexual nature.

First of all, he had to get himself an education. It is hard to comprehend how difficult this was in the late nineteenth century: there did exist scholarships at Oxford and Cambridge and at the emerging civic universities, but most secondary schools had not heard of them. For a boy in Wells's position, there was an almost total lack of information. (This was still true in my own time, born forty years later. I went to a grammar school which had, in a longish history, not once thought of producing a scholarship candidate.) By chance, by energy, and usually by some personal contact, occasionally boys like Wells emerged: but the amount of talent left unfulfilled doesn't bear thinking of.

He had two pieces of luck. During one of his apprenticeships, he was spotted by a local headmaster who knew a little science and who discovered that the boy could pass almost any kind of examination. With books on science—bad books by modern standards, but, as Hardy used to say, no book can be entirely bad that inspires the imagination of a clever boy—he set Wells going. The headmaster derived a reward somewhat odd but entirely deserved. For the Education Department (predecessor of the modern Department of Education and Science) had instituted a scheme of evening classes, and the teacher (in this case the headmaster) was paid quite substantial grants —in the terms of the 1880's—for students who could pass the subsequent examinations. The headmaster, through the skill of the young Wells, drew a nice addition to his income. His protégé was awarded by the Education Department the sum of one guinea a week to study at South Kensington. Some anonymous civil servant must have dreamed up that scheme, which was intended to select and train science teachers. It sounds primitive by the side of our articulated educational system, and yet it was more imaginative, more democratic, and more socially valuable than any piece of educational administration for years to come.

Wells at eighteen. The Normal School of Science (which we now know as the Royal College of Science, part of Imperial College). One guinea a week paid weekly on Wednesday (which meant, even in the mid-eighties, that he hadn't much to eat on Monday and Tuesday). For twelve months he was continuously happy. He said himself: "For a year I went shabby and grew shabbier. I was underfed and not very well housed, and it did not matter to me in the least because of the vision of life that was growing in my mind." He had had the second great piece of luck in his life. He was being taught zoology by T. H. Huxley.

Huxley was a great man. He was not, as a creative scientist, in the class of his friend Darwin: but then very few people are. He had a stronger, harder and less self-indulgent character than Darwin's. Darwin could not have wished for a more complementary and selfless ally: without him Darwin's work would have had a rougher and a longer ride before it got accepted. Huxley was one of the greatest of educators. More than any single man, he made an impact on Wells, who was himself to become the great educator of the next generation.

There was an uprush of excitement about late nineteenth century biology. The implications of evolutionary theory were driving in: it seemed that another major insight must be coming soon: everyone was waiting hopefully for the revelations which actually arrived sixty or seventy years later (they were dependent upon new techniques, in the eighties unimaginable). It was something like waiting for a Second Coming. Meanwhile, late nineteenth century physics was a dull subject. No one expected much from it. Many thought that it was effectively finished, and that it only remained to tidy up the pieces. It is a curious irony. The heroic age of physics was just on the point of starting. Meanwhile the biologists were braced on the balls of their feet. I remember A. C. Haddon telling me what it was like to be a biological student at that period. He was a few years older than Wells, became the first field anthropologist, and kept into his eighties a boyish enthusiasm for the days of Huxley, Francis Balfour and the other great teachers. "I used to *run* to my lectures," he said.

H. G. Wells ✻ 73

It was this devotion to science that Wells never lost. To the end of his life he wished he had become a professional scientist. If only he had gone straight on to research after that year under Huxley—if only the next two years had been as successful—he might have done "sound work" (one of his favorite phrases) in zoology. He might have added something to knowledge. He might have become a professor. Then, by the time we were talking, he would have been a professor emeritus, a title for which he had a singular fancy.

This sounds the kind of pose, half-nostalgic, half-falsified, that one sometimes meets in tycoons or politicians: wouldn't it have been pleasant to stay obscure? But I thought then, and still do, that there was more to it. He really believed in science—in its practical results, in its comprehension of the world. He was not a specially ambitious man. He did not get much fun, as Shaw did, out of being a public figure. He was extremely careless about his real gifts, and often did not seem to know what they were. No doubt he would have made a perfectly good professor of zoology, but it is extremely hard to think of him making a contribution like Pavlov's. He might easily have been as happy as in the life he actually led—except, one is obliged to remember, his sexual life, in the academic world of 1890 to 1930, would certainly have got him into trouble.

Whatever the truth of it, he often tried to impose his theoretical wishes on to me. Why wasn't I content to go back to physics? I might do "sound work" there. He wasn't ready to accept that I was, in a different fashion, as intransigent as he was himself. I ought to add that, though he did not tell me so, he probably had another motive in trying to persuade me. He didn't know whether my writing would turn out to be original enough. He liked *The Search,* but I suspect that he thought he could have done it better himself. When he read *Strangers and Brothers* in 1940, he wrote me a long letter. This was genuinely original, he said. He now accepted that I was right to change my career.

Well, he didn't become a professor. He had to take a series of inadequate jobs, teaching in private schools, correcting papers for that curious institution, the University Correspondence College, writing a zoology textbook, doing some journalism on the side. It was a life arduous enough for most young men: to make it a little more arduous, he had tuberculosis and an obscure kidney condition, and was thought likely to die. That did not deter him from taking a First Class degree in zoology in his off moments, nor from marrying. He seems to have allowed himself one single cry of self-pity. It would be bitter to die a virgin. Keats, another brave young man, cursed his fate in the same manner: but tuberculosis killed him, while Wells had got rid of the disease by his early thirties.

But it was his illness that pushed him into full-time writing. That was the only career where he could have his hemorrhages, long periods away from work, and still with luck make a living. So he settled down to produce a stream of articles (there were more markets for them in the nineties than there would have been seventy years later), and wrote *The Time Machine.*

He was, of course, a natural writer, as natural as Dickens. Whatever he touched, not only in writing, he had some inventive trick which made it his own and no one else's. But he had a gift more essential to a novelist than that. It was one he shared with Dickens, but I don't think he picked it up from Dickens as he did other, less primary things: it was the power to "realize" a scene without effort or strain, as though the trigger of involuntary memory had been pressed.

In the scientific romances, much the best yet written, this power was at its height: the actuality of the first chapter of *The War of the Worlds* is as complete as that of David Copperfield's first party. The same power was still in operation in *Mr. Britling Sees it Through,* not otherwise a good novel, written twenty years later. After that, it worked only fitfully, as Wells's interest in novel writing declined.

I don't pretend that there aren't loftier gifts which a novelist might hope to possess. But there is none more compelling. A writer can't learn it: he either has it or he hasn't: if he has it, people will read him; if he hasn't, they may admire but they won't read.

Henry James, with whom Wells had a long friendship, and who behaved more generously to Wells than Wells to him, used to puzzle about this mystery. Wells offended against the canons of James's aesthetics: he didn't in fact care whether canons existed or not: his novels were, according to James's standards, utterly uncomposed: and yet, James wrote wistfully: "I have read you, as I always read you, and as I read no one else, with a complete abdication of all those 'principles of criticism' . . . with which I roam, with which I totter, through the pages of others attended in some dim degree by the fond yet feeble theory of, but which I shake off, as I advance under your spell, with the most cynical inconsistency."

It was a great gift. It gained him instant recognition. As soon as *The Time Machine* and *The War of the Worlds* were published, he was known as a writer, he became comfortably off. His health improved. In 1900, when he was thirty-four, he was already started on his second public career, the one he thought more urgent than a novelist's, as the great educator of his time. The great educator of unlikely people, incidentally: "He is a seer," wrote Winston Churchill when he was a very old man.

It is no use regretting this. Wells could no more avoid teaching than Tolstoy could. It was part of him. If it hadn't been part of him, his best straight novels, *Tono-Bungay*, *Kipps*, *Mr. Polly*, would have been different books. But this didactic fiber—which, by the by, a number of the greatest artists have possessed—was, I think, strengthened by the tumults of his sexual life. He wanted, as most of us do, to justify himself. He wanted a society into which his life would fit. And that would take a pretty major transformation of society, for his life was a very odd one.

Like Dickens, whom he resembled in more ways than one, he was a man of strong sexuality. Like Dickens, in his early manhood he was a bad picker. He fell passionately in love with his cousin, who seems to have been a nice, simple girl. He married her, defying illness and penury—and then found that, though she was fond of him, she couldn't

H. G. Wells ※ 77

give him any response. As far as he was concerned, she was frigid. After a year or two Wells ran off with one of his students.

That all sounds in character, for an active, impatient man. But there were two singularities. The first was that he stayed in love with his cousin for years, long after they had been divorced and he had married his student. Somehow his cousin had captured his sexual imagination. The second was that his second wife, who was intelligent and charming and who looked after him until he died, also could not give him the kind of love he wanted.

So far the pattern is like Dickens's: for Dickens, after his years of a deadening marriage, broke it all up and went to Ellen Ternan—with whom he had a miserable time. But that happened when Dickens was middle-aged. Wells was still young at the time of his second marriage. He was also, underneath his Little Man comedy, a much more ruthless man than Dickens. He knew what he was going to take from life: he would get it only if he took it: he was just not going to be cheated. So his second wife became and remained a loving ally—it was a curious and touching relation—and Wells searched for joy, passion, love affairs, excitement, total love, elsewhere.

He searched, it should be said, with remarkable efficacy. He was nothing much to look at; he was short, and when his health established itself in his mid-thirties, he promptly became tubby. He was always slightly ashamed of his physique and of his squeaky voice. All he had to offer on the surface was a fine forehead, and beautiful, sad, unworldly, imaginative eyes. But he rapidly discovered that, as he liked to say, love can compel love: desire can certainly compel desire. He was great fun, a wonderful talker, he wanted women—it did not take long for women to want him.

As I remarked before, he was not born wise, but he learned much wisdom. He chose for his major loves (or they chose him) some of the most remarkable women of his time: one can trace the effect, not only of their attractiveness, but of their intelligence, in semi-autobiographical projections, such as *Ann Veronica, The New Machiavelli,* and *The World of William Clissold.* It was by any odds an unusual life: it aroused both the envy and the disapproval of his contemporaries: he paid no attention: he was set on wringing out of existence all that in his bitter youth he had dreamed of.

These complications—for, though it was an adventurous life, it was of course not an easy one—helped shape his vision of a new society and a new enlightenment: the new society would be founded on science: no one could stop it: poverty, hunger, the material miseries of the poor, were an insult to man's intelligence and would be swept away. A good deal of his social thinking reads quite fresh nowadays. And also, out of this scientific revolution would come a new enlightenment in which people would break free from sexual traditions and enjoy themselves far more gloriously. . . .

Those dots were a trick of his and look odd today: so does a lot of his emancipatory thinking. Yet, even though he was rationalizing his own life, some of it has come true in the western world: and certainly this part of his message, quite as much as the sober scientific foresight, made him an influence on the intelligent young for thirty years.

So much an influence, in fact, that most of his preaching will not be read again: it has sunk into the common assumptions. Some books of his, though, are being increasingly re-read: by a pleasing irony they are those which sparkle with those native gifts he took so lightly.

People have tried to disparage his social thinking by saying that he was optimistic: and since that is the harshest charge which can be brought against any modern writer, they think they need say no more. In fact, in the sense the criticism is intended, it is nonsense. Wells was about as much inclined to think men were naturally good, or naturally wise, as St. Augustine. His temperament forbade it: and if his temperament had not done so, his education would have. For, whatever evolutionary theory taught, it was not a belief in the survival value of the sweet and innocent. He *did* believe that, in man's crawl out from the caves up to the ramshackle society of 1900, the human species had acquired a bit more control over its own fate: and that it was no longer necessary for most of the human race to live hungry and die early. In his impatient fashion, he believed that this revolution could take place more quickly than it has done. If that is blind optimism, give us more of it.

His own sense of life was, in essence, dark. Unlike, say, Shaw's: but then Shaw, who was both a kinder and a colder man, had never had to struggle with a passionate nature. Wells was often more sanguine than most men: he was sanguine because he revelled in the joys of life: but in the end he had no illusions. This is manifest both in his very early books, like *The Time Machine* and *The Island of Dr. Moreau,* and in some late ones. Once again there is a parallel with Dickens. Mr. Bernard Bergonzi has recently had some interesting things to say about this aspect of Wells. But it wasn't all: it was present, but so was a passionate desire to teach, the faith that man could be educated, the ardent social hope.

When I knew him, he was already old: the dark shade was getting stronger: his bursts of intimacy had a knack of being lugubrious. I remember one night in 1938, when he came to Cambridge for the British Association meeting. He was giving a paper to the Education Section, and had been going about in the daytime in a London D.Sc. hood and cap, looking like one of his own little comic pictures. (He had recently gone to the labor of working out a thesis for his doctorate, just as though he had been a young academic. This seemed an extraordinary whim for a world figure: I shall suggest an explanation later.)

We finished the evening by sitting together in the lounge of the University Arms Hotel. It was late, well after midnight, and I have an idea that we were waiting for some acquaintances. Whatever the reason, we sat up, staring at the palms, a glass of whisky by each of our chairs. He had been saying that the only sharp difference he could see between my circle of friends in the thirties and his in the nineties was that mine drank much more. Untypically for him, the conversation tailed off. The silences got longer and longer. Without any introduction, he broke into the quiet. It was a simple question. He said:

"Ever thought of suicide, Snow?"

I reflected.

I said:

"Yes, H.G. I have."

He replied:

"So have I. But not till I was past seventy." He was then seventy-two. We drank some more whisky and looked somberly at the palms.

Part of that exchange seems not to have been true. He was a very honest man: but, like most of us, he was capable of speaking the truth of the moment rather than the truth of fact. In his autobiography (published four years before this conversation) he reported that he had contemplated suicide at sixteen: he was shut in the cul-de-sac misery of the draper's shop, and he went out at nights and studied the sea: it might be a better choice. As we sat in the hotel, he had forgotten that: the present was bleak enough.

He had plenty to depress him, both then and for the rest of his life. Not the war: he slept on the top floor of his Regent's Park house while the bombs were dropping, as calm as any man in London. But the joyous pleasures were finished. So was his influence: so were most of his hopes. He had mishandled his literary affairs, and he had lost his public. His professional vanity had never been deep, but it needed a little encouragement. He had just one personal ambition, and it was not going to be satisfied. Towards the end of the war, he began to die of cancer.

But he was too robust a man to be defeated all the time. At my last sight of him, he was as happy as I had seen him. It was the autumn of 1941: he went to Cambridge to take part in the commemoration of Comenius —who was one of the figures, like Roger Bacon and Machiavelli, with whom he liked to play at identifying himself. When he told me he was going, I decided to take a night off from war-time London, and I collected as many as I could of my younger friends. I thought that this was a chance, perhaps a last chance, that they ought not to miss.

H.G. (he liked being called so, particularly by the young) was in his gayest form. We gave him dinner in Christ's: the Master toasted him as the modern Comenius: H.G., with his usual lack of pomposity, squeaked that the modern Comenius would retire under the table. Then we went to my old rooms. He perched himself in an armchair by the fire, and we listened to him until the middle of the night.

He told me, as we went to bed, that he would have liked to make the young men talk: but that was not one of his talents, and anyone in his senses that night would have preferred just to keep him going. It is true that his hopes were failing: he said that he had given mankind the benefit of the doubt all his lifetime, but now mankind had better watch out. He said that with a kind of cockney impudence mixed with sadness. He was optimistic about the war, and his military judgments turned out right. As the night went on, his spirits became high. He was comic and prophetic, cantankerous and humorously poetic, exactly as in the dashing, careless books of his middle years. He would suddenly light up with a new piece of invention, throw out a phrase that crystallized a whole argument (at that particular verbal gift I had never heard anyone, and never have since, who was even remotely in the same class).

The next morning I heard his voice for the last time. We had got to bed about three, and I was sleeping soundly when I was awakened by heavy thumps at my bedroom door. "Gestapo! Gestapo!" H.G. was squeaking loudly. It was just after eight. He was up bright and early, and had come through from my spare room on his way to breakfast. "Off to see Waddy! Off to see Waddy!"

"Waddy" was my colleague, C. H. Waddington, the eminent biologist. It was the last word I heard H.G. utter. It was impossible to forget—partly because no one else, living or dead, has ever called Waddington by that singular name.

His last years were not enviable. Nor were the old ages of any of those I am writing about: all were harrowing to those close to them.* Wells's could have been lightened, if only for a day or two, by a small piece of administrative imagination. There was precisely one honor he longed for. It went back to his youth, when he daydreamed about being a scientist. He wanted to be an F.R.S. And this desire, instead of becoming weaker as he got older, became more obsessive. He felt, in increasing despondency, that it would justify his career. I am fairly sure, though it is guesswork, that this was the reason that he did laborious scholarship at seventy for his D.Sc. It was to prove that he could do reputable scientific work.

It may seem odd, or even slightly dotty, that he should want to be an F.R.S. If you are H. G. Wells, what can it conceivably matter? That was one of the arguments that some of my Royal Society friends used. The point was, it mattered to him. That should have been good enough. He had been the prophet of twentieth century

---

* Except perhaps Frost's. Neither Rutherford nor Hammarskjöld lived into old age.

science, more effectively than any man alive. It was shocking that the Royal Society should be so wooden.

Julian Huxley and other Biological Fellows did their best, but met blank resistance. I had no standing to take part in the controversy, being right outside the Society, but I argued with friends who were in it. Even from those I respected I got dim answers. The most respectable sounding was—the Royal Society is now restricted to people who have done scientific research and made original contributions to knowledge. Wells had done many more things, but he had not done that. Once we make an exception, even for him. . . .

The argument was reasonable and honorable, but it was not true. The Royal Society has always been in the habit of electing, every now and then, Cabinet Ministers and other dignitaries. It had elected Lord Hankey two or three years before this particular quarrel. It has elected several politicians and high officials since. All these non-scientific Fellows had done services to the state, true: their elections were grateful gestures, fine: but if them, why not Wells? I lost my temper. After twenty years, I still cannot remember those conversations without feeling angry all over again.

He was not elected. He lingered on and died at eighty. He had once told me, in his perky, defiant fashion: "Dying's a messy business, anyway." Yes, it was.

EINSTEIN

ONE day at Fenner's (the university cricket ground at Cambridge), just before the last war, G. H. Hardy and I were talking about Einstein. Hardy had met him several times, and I had recently returned from visiting him. Hardy was saying that in his lifetime there had only been two men in the world, in all the fields of human achievement, science, literature, politics, anything you like, who qualified for the Bradman class. For those not familiar with cricket, or with Hardy's personal idiom, I ought to mention that "the Bradman class" denoted the highest kind of excellence: it would include Shakespeare, Tolstoi, Newton, Archimedes, and maybe a dozen others. Well, said Hardy, there had only been two additions in his lifetime. One was Lenin and the other Einstein.

I wasn't quarreling with that. It was clear, all the theoretical physicists told us so, that if Einstein had not existed, twentieth century physics would itself have been different: this one could say of no one else, not even Rutherford or Bohr: to make that kind of difference was, incidentally, a necessary condition for entry into the Bradman class. Further, his character was inextricably mixed up with his achievement. Neither Hardy nor I were given to exaggerated estimates of human virtue: but again we took it for granted that, if the word "noble" had any meaning, this was the noblest man we had met.

Good, gentle and wise. Hardy recalled that some bright journalist had thrown off that description of Einstein: could I think of any three adjectives more exact? Here, for the first time, I began to hedge. Yes, they were true; but they didn't tell the whole truth, or anything like it. If one was talking in that kind of shorthand, one ought to add another adjective. But what should it be, without disturbing the impression? "Obstinate" was too weak and too carping, "counter-suggestible" was faintly grotesque, "independent" or "nonconformist" did not say anything like enough, "deliberately impersonal" was a half-truth. There was something in him that I couldn't describe but was stuttering towards. That conversation happened nearly thirty years ago, and, whenever I have thought about Einstein since, I have still found myself stuttering.

To begin with, he was much more unlike other men and women than the rest of those I am writing about. In psychological structure, though not of course in gifts, one can find plenty of parallels to Lloyd George, Rutherford, Wells, Hardy: most of us have met people bearing them a family resemblance in the course of our work-a-day lives. Churchill was much stranger. In some ways, I have come to think, there were faint likenesses between Churchill and Einstein. I don't mean that they were alike in terms of spirit or intellect: in those respects no one could bear comparison with Einstein. But in some aspects of their psychological nature, in the ways in which their characters formed themselves, I believe one can find some links. If I had thought of this while Hardy was alive, he would have repudiated me for good.

As with Churchill, there were some bizarre paradoxes in Einstein's career. I suspect that in natures like theirs, where the ego starts abnormally strong—though Einstein, unlike Churchill, learned to subjugate his personal self or forget it—these paradoxes are more likely to occur than with less inflexible men. Anyway, Einstein was universally recognized at thirty-seven as the greatest theoretical physicist of his age, the equal of Newton. That is still his ranking: the work he did between twenty-two and thirty-seven stands there for ever. But— It isn't that, like Newton, he gave up physics. It remained the prime internal devotion of his life, he worked at it with the ultimate concentration which was one of his supreme qualities until he died at seventy-six: and almost all his colleagues thought, and still think, that he wasted the second half of his life.

There were other paradoxes. He was the voice of liberal science, the prophet of reason and peace, for a generation. At the end, he believed, without bitterness, in the depth of his gentle and tranquil spirit, that it had all been in vain. He was the most complete of internationalists: he broke away from the Jewish community, he hated all separatisms and nationalisms: yet he was compelled to take his place as the most eminent Jew alive, the committed Zionist. He wanted to lose his personality in the world of nature; but that personality became one of the most publicized of the century, and his face—at first glance the face of an inspired and saintly gollywog—as well known as a film star's.

Just to add to the list, he was credited, or blamed, with a paradox that did not exist. It has become a legend that he was responsible for the atomic bomb—that he, the prophet of human brotherhood, had to take on his conscience the slaughter of Hiroshima and Nagasaki, and the possibility of genocides to come. It would have been an irony, but it was not true. In practice, the discovery of nuclear fission owed nothing to his work: and his part in sending the famous letter to Roosevelt in 1939 was not significant. I will try to de-personalize this story a little later.

It was, of course, his moral character which demonstrated itself in those paradoxes of his life. That character was already formed before he was sixteen. Here we have to rely on the facts (his career is unusually well documented, especially through Swiss sources) and to take his own comments, written when he was an old man, as rationalizations after the event.

I have never belonged whole-heartedly to a country, a state, nor to a circle of friends, nor even to my own family.

My personal external circumstances played only a minor role in my thoughts and my emotions.

Perception of this world by thought, leaving out everything subjective, became, partly consciously, partly unconsciously, my supreme aim. [Of himself, in early adolescence.]

When I was still a rather precocious young man, I already realized most vividly the futility of the hopes and aspirations that most men pursue throughout their lives.

Well-being and happiness never appeared to me as an absolute aim. I am even inclined to compare such moral aims to the ambitions of a pig.

Those statements (which came from the bone of his character, and altogether omit the jolly, laughing flesh) were written in old age. They couldn't have been made by many men—perhaps by Spinoza, whom Einstein so much admired and in spirit resembled. But, even from Spinoza or Einstein, they need a bit of understanding. After all, these men did live on this earth like the rest of us.

Einstein's family were easy-going, free-thinking petit-bourgeois, whose ancestors had lived in Swabia for generations. They were Jewish by origin, but agnostic and indifferent to religion. It was a tolerant and casual home: uncomfortably casual insomuch as his father, who started a small electrical factory in Munich when Einstein was one year old (in 1880), did not have the drive to make a go of it. But they were never really poor, as the Wellses and the Rutherfords were.

The young Einstein was not a brilliant child. Intellectually, he seemed backward (this was also true of Churchill). He was late in learning to talk. All this is singular, particularly so for a future mathematician. As a rule, mathematical talent shows itself at a very early age. A high proportion of eminent mathematicians have asked questions about large or infinite numbers before they were three: the stories about Hardy and Dirac, for example, are well authenticated. The only really good juvenile mathematician I have personally watched was in good form at the age of four. Now we are beginning to learn more about this sharp and specific talent, I believe that we shall normally know whether children do or do not possess it before they have learned to read.

Well, Einstein was not a mathematician in the sense Hardy was, but no one would suggest that he was devoid of mathematical ability. Little or none of this was detected in his early childhood. He did begin, at the age of ten, to show precocity: but it was a precocity, not of intellect, but of character.

His parents, who might have been Catholic converts if they had had any religion at all, sent him first to a Catholic primary school. That he didn't mind. At ten he went on to one of the Munich gymnasia. That he hated: and he hated it for just the same reasons as he would have hated it at seventy. It was militaristic: at once, and for ever, he detested German militarism. Children marched and drilled: teachers barked: it was a barracks. In later life he became as unqualified a nonconformist as a man can be. He often rationalized his actions, but they deserve some inspection. At ten he was already certain that this disciplined machine was not for him. He had a horror of constraint, in any shape or form, physical, emotional, intellectual. *Zwang*. Did I know the German word, he asked me, as we talked about English manners. In the Munich high school he made his first strike against *Zwang*.

He did, in fact, both a brave and an odd thing. He became, for a short period, about a year, a religious Jew. It was an attempt, as he saw it later, to "liberate himself from purely personal links." It was also an attempt to mark himself out from the conformity which surrounded him. As we shall see, he repeated this pattern at the height of his fame: when, without belief, he once more stamped himself as a Jew, an active Zionist. If he was going to be identified with any group—and that was difficult, so unyielding was his ego—then it must be with the poor and persecuted of the world.

This decision, like each single decision that he took in his life, came from within himself. At ten he seems to have rested as much certainty in his own thought as he did at seventy: his own thought, and that of no one else alive. The religious phase did not last long. Once more he applied his own thought to it: and at twelve he emerged into the kind of cosmic religious non-belief which lasted him a lifetime. He used the word "God" so often that people were often deceived. From his boyhood he possessed deep religious *feeling*: but when he spoke of God, he did not mean what a religious believer means (although he might perhaps have accepted Bonhoeffer's God). As he said himself in middle-age: "I believe in Spinoza's God who reveals himself in the harmony of all being, not in a God who concerns himself with the fate and actions of men."

That conclusion he reached in early adolescence, brooding by himself as a pupil—not at all a distinguished one—at the Munich high school. With the same total independence he decided what to work at. He was quite good, no more, at physics and mathematics. Most of the academic drill struck him as intolerable, and he would not play. In this he was quite unlike most clever boys and nearly all future academics. People like Rutherford (who was as original in creative power, though not in temperament) took what they were given and made the best of it. Hardy disliked Winchester, but was a born competitor who wanted the prizes and the Trinity scholarship. To Einstein competition meant nothing: he had no temptation to compromise or please. Here again one can see a ghostly resemblance to the young Churchill, unable or unwilling to make a serious effort at school, except at writing English essays, which he happened to enjoy.

Einstein's father was a peculiarly unsuccessful businessman. The Munich business was a flop, and so, more or less absent-mindedly, he moved on to Milan, where he did slightly worse. This move happened when Einstein was fifteen; he was left behind in Munich to complete his schooling. Since his mind had been totally independent before, it could not become more so: but he had six months alone and reached three more solitary decisions.

He arrived in Milan and announced them to a family which seems to have been as cheerful about them as he was himself. The first was to leave the Munich school, which he hated, and to abandon the final examination, which he despised. The second was to leave the Jewish community, to which he still formally belonged. The third, and the most dramatic, was to give up his German citizenship. He decided to have no obligations which he did not make himself. His moral confidence was absolute. He was enough, just on his own.

As an anti-climax, he promptly failed his entrance examination to the Zurich Polytechnic. He wanted to study there, in order to become an electrical engineer—which sounds quaint, because of the legend of Einstein's unpracticality: in fact he was no more unpractical than Hardy was absent-minded: these cheap stereotypes are hard to destroy. Although Einstein's father could not find a franc, better-off members of the Einstein family—scattered all over Europe in the Jewish wanderings—thought a Zurich education might not be a bad idea, and were prepared to scrape an allowance for him until he graduated. Not entirely surprisingly, he passed the entrance examination in the subjects he had studied, and failed in those he had not.

So he, already mature to an extent most men never achieve, had to put in a year in a Swiss cantonal school, and, with a trace of cussedness, enjoyed it. From there he duly passed into Zurich, now intending to train as a physics teacher. As usual, he immediately came into opposition with *Zwang*. Not that he didn't like the Swiss, who, in his view, were civilized and democratic. This time *Zwang* cropped up in the shape of examinations. The curriculum could have been better devised, thought Einstein. The examinations so constrained his mind, that, when he had graduated, he did not want to think about scientific problems for a year.

Actually, he was quite lucky. He was taught by one man of genius, Minkowski, who later recognized, after Einstein's early publications, that his pupil was a much greater genius (but as a student "a lazy dog"). The general standard of the Zurich Polytechnic was high. He made friends who thought that he was a superior being. He was probably as well off at Zurich as he would have been at Hardy's Cambridge.

The truth was, no university in the nineties could have contained or satisfied him—and it is doubtful whether any university could satisfy a young Einstein today. He was beyond the normal limits of independence.

He passed his final examination all right, though not spectacularly. But Zurich did not keep him on as an assistant (i.e., the lowest grade of post-graduate job). That was a gross error in talent-spotting: it was almost the only misadventure which rankled with him. And yet, at almost exactly the same time, Cambridge failed to keep the much more accommodating Rutherford, who, instead of being given a fellowship, was encouraged to remove himself to Montreal.

So Einstein was a graduate, but unemployed. For a while it looked as though he was unemployable. He took one or two temporary teaching posts. He had no money at all. The Einstein clan had financed his education, but now they expected him to earn a living. He had one old suit, which didn't matter, and little food, which did. He was rescued by a generous and admiring friend, Marcel Grossman, who became himself a good scientist. Grossman persuaded his father, a well-to-do Swiss industrialist, to recommend Einstein for a position.

The position was, of all extraordinary things, that of patent examiner in the Swiss Federal Patent Office. As an even more extraordinary thing, Einstein was appointed. The job was not specially arduous, and Einstein turned out to be good at it. One of his greatest intellectual gifts, in small matters as well as great, was to strip off the irrelevant frills from a problem: that happens to be the prime gift of a good patent examiner. He was also, as I have said, not at all devoid of practical sense. He liked gadgets, understood them, and even tried to invent them himself. Thus he did his patent work at great speed, efficiently, soon got extra pay, and was left, at twenty-three, with time to meditate: which for him meant time to meditate, day after day, night after night, week after week, with the kind of concentration which was like a man grasping an object in his fist, on the nature of the physical universe.

He needed only one resource, which was his own insight. His thinking, of course, carried abstraction very far, but it is important to realize that his insight was first and foremost a *physical* one. At Zurich he had spent most of his time in the physics laboratory. When he did much of his major work his knowledge of mathematics was, by the standard of the top theoretical physicists, thin and patchy: he was much less well equipped than Clerk Maxwell, Born, Heisenberg, Pauli: to an extent, he had to pick up his mathematics as he went along, for the rest of his career. He said himself: ". . . my intuition in the mathematical field was not strong enough to be able to distinguish with basic conviction the fundamentally important from the rest of the more or less dispensable erudition. Moreover, my interest in acquiring a knowledge of Nature was infinitely stronger, and as a student it was not clear to me that the approach to a deeper knowledge of the principles of physics was bound up with the most intricate mathematical methods. This only dawned on me after years of independent scientific work."

It only dawned on him, in fact, when his physical insight had already led him to solve some of the great problems: when the special theory of relativity was behind him, and he was brooding on the general one: it was then he saw that the physical insight had to be interwoven with the heavy machinery of the tensor calculus.

It was like him to begin his work—and to achieve more than most mathematical physicists in a lifetime—with the aid of nothing but his own pure unaided thought. No one else would have started with that suspicion of mathematical techniques. At twenty-three he was already the man whom the world later wished, but had failed, to understand. He had absolute confidence. He had absolute faith in his own insight. He was set on submerging his personality, for good and all, in the marvels of the natural world.

No one has stripped away the claims of self more ruthlessly, not even Niels Bohr, another of the saints of science. But it is wrong to romanticize anyone, even Einstein. It seems to me that a man has to possess a pretty hefty ego to need to subdue it so totally. A more naturally self-forgetful man wouldn't have required such a moral effort to forget himself. He did it: perhaps that was why, when I met him, I felt that he had been shaped by moral experience. It is here that one can pick out the black and white difference from Churchill, a similarly structured personality. Churchill too had a pretty hefty ego: but he didn't submerge it or even try to, he simply let it rip. It was probably only in action that he felt the same impersonality into which, by a moral imperative, Einstein serenely made himself.

But the old-Adam-ego was not quite drowned. I think one ought to be a little wary of his attitude to the conventions. Yes, no one has been less conventional: but his rationalizations were somewhat too masterly. Somehow a man isn't so totally unconventional as that if he is absolutely free. It's easier sometimes to wear socks, even if other people have the habit of wearing socks, than to explain that socks get holes in them. It takes too much effort to question each social action. Free-and-easy people take the conventions more lightly, sometimes dropping them, sometimes drifting along. It's more convenient, I should have thought, to get into a dinner jacket than to hack away at shirt-sleeves with a razor in order to make a kind of under-vest: but Einstein would firmly have thought the opposite. About him, even in Jehovianic old age, there was still a residue—no, not really a residue but a vestigial air—of a nonconformer from a central European café, the sort of character one used to meet between the wars, who made an impact by wearing odd shoes and his coat on backwards.

As a very young man, when he was producing great discoveries, Einstein's only society was in just those cafés. He was the least gregarious of humankind—he spoke of his own "unconcealed lack of the need to frequent my fellow human beings and human communities." Yet he enjoyed the desultory easy-going European nights, the cigars, the coffee, the talk; he was both witty and merry, he had a reverberating laugh, he didn't give a damn. When life had sobered him, when he felt responsibility for so much, he missed those nights. He never got used to American parties, where people drank hard and didn't want to argue about ultimates. So far as he was ever at home, at any time in his life, it was in Berne and Zurich before the First World War.

He got married in Berne, as soon as he took on his job at the Patent Office there. About this marriage, and his first wife, there is a conflict of evidence: much of the biographical material is good (there is a specially attractive one by Antonia Vallentin), but here there is some factual mystery. This first wife was a fellow-student at Zurich, four years older than he was: she was a Serbian called Mileva Maric. Here the certainty stops. She seems to have had a limp. Most of Einstein's Swiss contemporaries thought she was gloomy and incompetent; she may have been a genuine depressive. None of this sounds alluring, but other reports give her a Slav nakedness to life, a defenseless charm.

Was the marriage unhappy from the beginning? This will presumably never be known, though I picked up what may have been a clue. Einstein was utterly reticent about his personal life: a "puritanical reserve" was necessary, he said, to a scientist seeking truth. Antonia Vallentin, who knew his second wife well, suggests that he was a man of powerful sensuality. When I met him, that was certainly one of the impressions that he gave: but it is entirely possible, and perhaps more probable than possible, that he, like Tolstoi and Gandhi, both of whom he revered, felt that his sensuality was one of the chains of personality that ought to be slipped off. Anyway, in his first marriage he soon had two sons—those two he certainly loved. The older gave him no trouble, and in due course became an excellent engineering professor in California. The younger one seems to have inherited, in an acute form, his mother's melancholia, and brought Einstein in middle-age what was perhaps his deepest private grief.

Meanwhile, his first child born, Einstein, twenty-six years old, only three years away from crude privation, still a patent examiner, published in the *Annalen der*

Physik in 1905 five papers on entirely different subjects. Three of them were among the greatest in the history of physics. One, very simple, gave the quantum explanation of the photoelectric effect—it was this work for which, sixteen years later, he was awarded the Nobel Prize. Another dealt with the phenomenon of Brownian motion, the apparently erratic movement of tiny particles suspended in a liquid: Einstein showed that these movements satisfied a clear statistical law. This was like a conjuring trick, easy when explained: before it, decent scientists could still doubt the concrete existence of atoms and molecules: this paper was as near to a direct proof as a theoretician could give. The third paper was the special theory of relativity, which quietly amalgamated space, time and matter into one fundamental unity.

This last paper contains no references and quotes no authority. All the papers are written in a style unlike any other theoretical physicist's. They contain very little mathematics. There is a good deal of verbal commentary. The conclusions, the bizarre conclusions, emerge as though with the greatest of ease: the reasoning is unbreakable. It looks as though he had reached the conclusions by pure thought, unaided, without listening to the opinions of others. To a surprisingly large extent, that is precisely what he had done.

It is pretty safe to say that, so long as physics lasts, no one will again hack out three major break-throughs in one year. People have complained that Einstein was not immediately recognized. This seems mildly unrealistic. Within a few months physicists at Cracow were saying that a new Copernicus had been born. It took about four years for the top German physicists, such as Planck, Nernst and von Laue, to begin proclaiming that he was a genius. In 1909, before he had any academic job at all, he was given an honorary degree at Geneva. Just afterwards Zurich University (not the Polytechnic) offered him a professorship. In 1911 he went to a full chair at the German University in Prague. In 1912 he was recalled to the Zurich Polytechnic, which had had, only a dozen years before, no use for him. In 1913 he was elected to the Prussian Academy of Science, at a high salary for those days, to be left free in Berlin for no duties except his research. He was by then thirty-four. He was being treated as handsomely as any scientist alive. I don't think the academic community, in particular the German-speaking academic community, comes out of that story badly.

There was, however, trouble in his home. No one knows how deeply it affected him. By the time he had moved to Prague, his marriage was going wrong. Altogether, the stay in Prague was an unhappy one. Einstein had to become a state official of the Hapsburg Empire, in order to do which he had to declare his religion. He had lost all connections with Judaism: but anti-semitism was strong in Austria, and that was enough reason for Einstein to insist on registering himself—Israelite. His wife, Mileva, was sunk in melancholia: it didn't help that she was a Slav, in the midst of racial unrest.

Yet Einstein's laugh was still ringing out, his spirits were not yet damped. He was showing a new ability as an actor—with a touch of ham—on the lecture platform. There are pleasant stories of his playing the violin to a cultivated salon which discussed Kant, Hegel and Fichte and played chamber music. The party often included Franz Kafka, not yet known to fame. One wonders if they ever talked to each other. They would not have had much in common.

When he went to Berlin in 1914, he left his wife and sons in Zurich. The marriage was over: he must have known it, though it seems that he did not say it. He was overcome by sadness, of a kind rare in him, when he left his sons.

He arrived in Berlin some months before war broke out. He was already famous in the scientific world. He was going to attract fame in the world outside such as no scientist has known before or since. He was a pacifist soon forced to watch what he regarded as German madness among, not only the crowd, but his fellow-members of the Academy. He had preserved his Swiss nationality, which was some sort of protection, when, with his habitual courage, he became an ally of Romain Rolland. But he soon came to experience the blackest unpopularity. He could shrug it off: "Even the scientists of various countries behave as though eight months ago [he was writing to Rolland in May 1915] they had had their brains amputated."

Nevertheless, in the middle of militaristic tumult, he found both personal and creative peace. Perhaps, or probably, the two were connected. Anyway, he went to live in Berlin with one of his uncles: and with this uncle's daughter, who had been unsatisfactorily married, divorced, and had two small daughters, he was happy. Maybe he fell in love: but, once again, this is unknown. Certainly he wanted no one else. When he was himself divorced, some years later, he married her. She protected him from nuisances until he died. She was unexacting, she was high-spirited, she was fun, she was shrewd about people. Unlike his first wife, who was trained as a mathematician, she knew nothing whatever about his work. It was the kind of marriage that some of the greatest scientists have made. It set him free, and left him free. Before he met her, he had been going through a fallow period scientifically. Almost immediately after, he was thinking with a concentration, and reaching a creative ecstasy more intense than he had known.

In November 1915 he wrote to Arnold Sommerfeld, himself a fine physicist, one of the classical scientific letters: "This last month I have lived through the most exciting and the most exacting period of my life: and it would be true to say that it has also been the most fruitful. Writing letters has been out of the question. I realize that up till now my field equations of gravitation have been entirely devoid of foundation. When all my confidence in the old theory vanished, I saw clearly that a satisfactory solution could only be reached by linking it with the Riemann variations. The wonderful thing that happened then was that not only did Newton's theory result from it, *as a first approximation*, but also the perihelion motion of mercury, *as a second approximation*.* For the deviation of light by the sun I obtain twice the former amount."

Sommerfeld wrote a cautious and sceptical reply.

* The perihelion motion of mercury had already been measured, but not explained. The measurement agreed exactly with that which was required by Einstein's theory. Einstein was also predicting another very small optical effect which in 1916 had not yet been measured.

Einstein sent him a postcard: "You will become con-vinced of the general theory of relativity as soon as you have studied it. Therefore I shall not utter a word in its defense."

It did not need defense. It was published in 1916. As soon as it reached England—across the increasing harsh-ness of the war—scientists thought that it was almost cer-tainly right. The greatest revolution in thought since Newton, they were saying. As a consequence of his theory (see previous footnote), Einstein had made a prediction. It was the prediction of an experimental effect which astronomers could test. In his paper, he asked them to do so. The English astronomers decided that this should be done. In March 1917—again across the war—they an-nounced that on March 29, 1919, a total eclipse of the sun was taking place. The critical experiment must be set up and Einstein's theory tested.

That is an old story. The test, of course, came out as predicted, and Einstein's theory stood.

It is a strange theory. As with Rutherford, as with most scientists, if Einstein had never lived most of his work would soon have been done by someone else, and in much the same form. He said himself that that was true of the special theory of relativity. But, when he general-ized the special theory so as to include the gravitational field, he did something that might not have been done for generations: and, above all, might not have been done in that way. It might, some good theoreticians have sug-gested, have ultimately been done in a way easier for others to handle. It remains an extraordinary monolith, like a Henry Moore sculpture, which he alone could have constructed—and at which he himself hacked away, hoping to make something grander, for the rest of his scientific life.

I will return in a moment to the second half of his scientific life, which was at the same time extraordinary, unsuccessful, and profoundly characteristic. In the meantime his public life, as soon as the general theory was published (his fame had already mounted *before* the confirmation), was unlike that which any other scientist is likely to experience again. No one knows quite why, but he sprang into the public consciousness, all over the world, as the symbol of science, the master of the twentieth century intellect, to a large extent the spokesman for human hope. It seemed that, perhaps as a release from the war, people wanted a human being to revere. It is true that they did not understand what they were revering. Never mind, they believed that here was someone of supreme, if mysterious, excellence.

As a symbol of science, either Rutherford or Niels Bohr might have been chosen. Rutherford left a more direct mark on twentieth century science (Einstein said: "I consider Rutherford to be one of the greatest experimental scientists of all time, and in the same class as Faraday. The reason I had no opportunity of mentioning him in my writings is because I concentrated on speculative theories, whereas Rutherford managed to reach profound conclusions on the basis of almost primitive reflection combined with relatively simple experimental methods.") Bohr founded a great Socratic school of theoretical physicists, and influenced others as Einstein never did. Both Rutherford and Bohr were good men, but Rutherford hadn't Einstein's moral independence or resource: Bohr may have had, but could not project it. No, the public instinct was correct. As Hardy used to quote—it's only the highbrows (in the unpleasant sense) who do not admire the real swells.

Throughout the twenties he made himself the champion of good causes. He became a Zionist, though his religious thinking was quite un-Judaic: * he was on the side of Zion, out of an ultimate loyalty and also, as I have said before, because the Jews were the insulted and injured of this world. He spent a lot of time trying to promote international pacifism. This sounds strange to us now, but the twenties was a period of ideals, and even Einstein, the least suggestible of men, shared them. At a later period of his life, some Americans used to call him naïve. This made me cross: he was not at all naïve: what they meant was that he didn't think that the United States was always 100 per cent right, and the Soviet Union 100 per cent wrong.

If they had studied his public attitudes they might— but they couldn't, reason had gone to sleep—have realized that he had always stood above the battles. He could not have become a partisan if he had tried. In one sense, he was totally detached. In another, he felt an absolute duty to his fellow-men. Antonia Vallentin says with accuracy that spiritually he was free of all chains, but morally he was bound by them. He loved his solitude—"painful when one is young, but delightful when one is more mature": but still, the more so as he became world-famous, he knew his duty. "The concern for man and his destiny must always be the chief interest of all technical effort.

* To a Gentile, his moral thinking often seemed strongly Judaic.

Never forget it among your diagrams and equations." Later he said: "Only a life lived for others is worth while."

In the twenties life had still not quite sobered him. He went about the world, sockless, rather like an itinerant musician. Everyone, including himself, complained about the ordeals of publicity. Here, for once, I register a dissenting vote. There was a streak in him, major prophet though he was, which enjoyed the photographers and the crowds. He had an element, as I have indicated before, of the exhibitionist and the ham, coexisting with his spiritual grandeur. If there had not been that element, there would have been no photographers and no crowds. Nothing is easier to avoid than publicity. If one genuinely doesn't want it, one doesn't get it. Einstein was under no compulsion to travel round the world. If he had retired—it would have been perfectly practicable—to his birthplace in Swabia, he could have revelled in obscurity.

But he didn't. Some of his remarks about publicity in the twenties sounded, as usual, like the Old Testament. But—much more than we think in our rationalizations— what you want is what happens to you.

That wasn't true, though, on the world scene. He had always been more realistic than most men about German politics: he knew the violent seething underneath the Weimar state. As soon as Hitler took the power, Einstein was quicker than any politician to judge what was going to happen. International pacificism, the world community, intellectual cooperation—all his hopes had to be put aside. He was much more rapid than Churchill in recognizing that the Nazi Reich had to be put down by force.

He was himself Hitler's greatest public enemy. He was out of Germany when Hitler became Chancellor: he was a brave man, but he knew that if he returned he would be killed. Through most of 1933 he lived in the little Flemish seaside town of Den Haan (Coq-sur-mer). There he kept a kind of intellectual court for refugees. Den Haan was temporarily the capital of the German-speaking scientific world. Incidentally, it is the most agreeable village on the Flanders coast, and they have a pleasant custom of naming streets after great men—Shakespeare laan, Dante laan, Rembrandt laan, and so on. But they haven't yet named a street after their most illustrious resident.

Belgium suited him. He was more comfortable in small cozy countries (Holland was his favorite), but he wasn't safe from the Nazis. Unwillingly he set off on his travels again, went to Princeton, and stayed there until he died.

It was a kind of exile. There is no doubt that he, who had never recognized any place as home, sometimes longed for the sounds and smells of Europe. Nevertheless it was in America that he reached his full wisdom and his full sadness. His wife died soon after he got there. His younger son, back in Switzerland, had gone into a mental home. His merriness had finally been worn away. He was left with his duty to other men.

He was left with something else, too. He could still lose his personality, forget everything else, in speculating about the natural world. That was the deepest root of his existence: it remained strong until the night before he died. He once said in public: "Whoever finds a thought which enables us to obtain a slightly deeper glimpse into the eternal secrets of nature, has been given great grace." He continued—this was the grace of his solitariness—to try to find such thoughts. Quite unlike Newton, who gave up physics entirely in order to become Master of the Mint and perform textual researches on the Bible, Einstein stayed working at science long after most theoreticians, even the best, have taken to something easier. But he worked—and this was the final strangeness of his life—in a direction flat opposite to that of his major colleagues. In the public world, against militarism, against Hitler, against cruelty and unreason, nothing had ever made him budge. In the private world of theoretical physics, with the same quiet but total intransigence, he would not budge against the combined forces of the colleagues he loved, Bohr, Born, Dirac, Heisenberg, the major intellects in his own profession.

They believed that the fundamental laws were statistical—that, when it came to quantum phenomena, in Einstein's picturesque phrase, God had to play at dice. He believed in classical determinism—that, in the long run, it should be possible to frame one great field theory in which the traditional concept of causality would re-emerge. Year after year he explained and re-defined his position.

To Carl Seelig: "I differ decisively in my opinions about the fundamentals of physics from nearly all my contemporaries, and therefore I cannot allow myself to act as spokesman for theoretical physicists. In particular I do not believe in the necessity for a statistical formulation of the laws."

To Max Born: "I can quite well understand why you

take me for an obstinate old sinner, but I feel clearly that you do not understand how I came to travel my lonely way. It would certainly amuse you, although it would be impossible for you to appreciate my attitude. I should also have great pleasure in tearing to pieces your positivistic-philosophical viewpoint."

To James Franck: "I can, if the worst comes to the worst, still realize that God may have created a world in which there are no natural laws. In short, a chaos. But that there should be statistical laws with definite solutions, i.e., laws which compel God to throw the dice in each individual case, I find highly disagreeable."

God does *not* play at dice, he kept saying. But, though he worked at it for nearly forty years, he never discovered his unified field theory. And it is true that his colleagues, who passionately venerated him, sometimes thought that he was "an obstinate old sinner." They believed that he had misspent half the mental lifetime of the most powerful intellect alive. They felt they had lost their natural leader.

The arguments on both sides are most beautiful and subtle. Unfortunately they cannot be followed without some background of physics: otherwise Bohr's *Discussion on Epistemological Problems* and Einstein's *Reply* ought to be part of everyone's education. No more profound intellectual debate has ever been conducted—and, since they were both men of the loftiest spirit, it was conducted with noble feeling on both sides. If two men are going to disagree, on the subject of most ultimate concern to them both, then that is the way to do it. It is a pity that the debate, because of its nature, can't be common currency.

Perhaps I can, by an analogy, suggest the effect on Einstein's colleagues of his one-man counter-revolution. It was rather as though Picasso, about 1920, at the height of his powers, had announced that some new kind of representational painting alone could be made to contain the visual truth: and had spent the rest of his life industriously but unavailingly trying to find it.

The great debate did not reach its peak until Einstein was old, years after the war. It was never resolved. He and Bohr, with mutual admiration, drew intellectually further apart. In fact, though, when I met Einstein in 1937 he had already separated himself totally, and as it proved finally, from the other theorists.

I had already shaken hands with him once or twice at large gatherings. That summer I happened to be in America, and my friend Leopold Infeld, who was collaborating with Einstein at the time, suggested that I might like to spend a day with him.

It turned out to be an abnormally hot day, even for a New York summer. The seats were hot in the car, as Infeld, a woman friend and I drove out to Long Island. We had a snack by way of lunch, and aimed at arriving at one o'clock. Actually we turned up late. Einstein had taken this house for the summer, since sailing remained one of his continuing pleasures. Infeld had not been there: no one in the neighborhood knew where Einstein was living, nor apparently had the slightest idea who he was. Infeld, not the most patient of men, was getting distinctly ratty. We had no telephone number. Finally we had to ring back to Princeton, track down one of the Institute's secretaries (which wasn't easy, because it was either a Saturday or a

Sunday) and get directions. At last we made it, three-quarters of an hour late.

Not that that mattered to Einstein. He was amiable to all visitors, and I was just one of many. He came into the sitting room a minute or two after we arrived. There was no furniture apart from some garden chairs and a small table. The window looked out on to the water, but the shutters were half-closed to keep out the heat. The humidity was very high.

At close quarters Einstein's head was as I had imagined it: magnificent, with a humanizing touch of the comic. Great furrowed forehead: aureole of white hair: enormous, bulging, chocolate-brown eyes. I can't guess what I should have expected from such a face if I hadn't known. A shrewd Swiss once said it had the brightness of a good artisan's countenance, that he looked like a reliable, old-fashioned watchmaker in a small town who perhaps collected butterflies on a Sunday.

What did surprise me was his physique. He had come in from sailing and was wearing nothing but a pair of shorts. It was a massive body, very heavily muscled: he was running to fat round the midriff and in the upper arms, rather like a footballer in middle-age, but he was still an unusually strong man. All through his life he must have had much greater physical strength than any of the others I am writing about. He was cordial, simple, utterly unshy: the large eyes looked at me, as though he was thinking: what had I come for, what did I want to talk about? Infeld, not only a man of distinguished intellect, but sharp-witted, set to work to find topics, as he went on doing through the afternoon and evening ahead. I was a friend of G. H. Hardy, Infeld began. Einstein smiled with pleasure. Yes, a fine man. Then, quite sharply, he asked me: was Hardy still a pacifist? I replied, as near as made no matter.

"I do not understand," he said somberly, "how such a fine man can be so unrealistic."

Then he wanted to know if I also was a pacifist. Far from it, I explained. I was by that time certain that war was inevitable. I was not so much apprehensive about war, as about the chance that we might lose it. Einstein nodded. About politics that afternoon, he and I and Infeld were united. About politics in the widest sense, I don't think there has been a world figure in my time who has been wiser than Einstein. He wasn't much interested in political techniques, and brushed them off too lightly: but his major insights into the world situation, and his major prophecies, have proved more truthful than those of anyone else.

The hours went on. I have a hazy memory that several people drifted in and out of the room, but I do not remember who they were. Stifling heat. There appeared to be no set time for meals. He was already, I think, eating very little, but he was still smoking his pipe. Trays of open sandwiches—various kinds of wurst, cheese, cucumber—came in every now and then. It was all casual and Central European. We drank nothing but soda water. What with the heat and the sandwiches I got as thirsty as if I had been dehydrated, and drank more soda water in eight hours than I normally did in eight months.

Mostly we talked of politics, the moral and practical choices in front of us, and what could be saved from the storm to come, not only for Europe but for the human race. All the time he was speaking with a weight of moral experience which was different, not only in quantity but in kind, from anything I had met. By this time he had lost any intrusion from his own ego, as though it had never existed. It was something like talking to the second Isaiah.

It would be easy to give a false impression. In the face of someone so different from the rest of us, it was hard not to get one. In fact, he was neither sentimental nor illusioned. His view of life was not illusioned at all. It was far darker than that of his great friend Paul Langevin. Einstein thought that we should be lucky if the human race was going to stand a chance: but nevertheless, as an absolute moral imperative, we had to do what little we could until we dropped.

Infeld, who knew him better than anyone at this period, later wrote—and it seems to me precisely true:

This "conscience of the world" [Einstein] nurses a deep repugnance for all types of boastfulness, terrorizing of one's fellow-men and overbearing brutality. One could, therefore, easily have been tempted to portray him as an over-sensitive man, who trembles at the very mention of injustice and violence. This picture would be utterly false. I know no one who leads such a lonely and solitary life as he. His great benevolence, his absolute integrity and his social ideas, despite all appearances to the contrary, are thoroughly impersonal and seem to come from another planet. His heart does not bleed, his eyes do not weep.

And yet, he had suffered much, in a way difficult for more ego-bound men to understand. I had heard a lot of his old merriness. That had all disappeared, and for ever. Just once in eight hours I heard the great laugh of his young manhood come rumbling out. It was at a curious turn in the conversation. He had been speaking of the countries he had lived in. He preferred them, he said, in inverse proportion to their size. How did he like England, I asked. Yes, he liked England. It had some of the qualities of his beloved Holland. After all, by world standards, England was becoming a small country. We talked of the people he had met, not only of the scientists but the politicians. Churchill. Einstein admired him. I said that progressives of my kind wanted him in the government as a token of resistance: this was being opposed, not so much by the Labor Party, but by Churchill's own Tories. Einstein was brooding. To defeat Nazism, he said, we should need every kind of force, including nationalism, that we could bring together.

Then, because there wasn't much useful to say, I asked why, when he left Germany, he hadn't come to live in England.

"No, no!" said Einstein.

Why not?

"It is your style of life." Suddenly he had begun to laugh. "It is a splendid style of life. But it is not for me."

He was enjoying some gigantic joke. But I was puzzled. What was this mysterious "style of life?" It appeared that, on his first day in England, he had been taken to a great country house. A butler. Evening dress. Einstein had never worn a dinner jacket in his life. Then Lindemann had taken him in to dinner at Christ Church. More butlers. More evening dress. Einstein chortled. He seemed to have the fixed idea that the English, or certainly the English professional classes, spend much of their time getting in and out of formal clothes. Any protests I made (did he think Hardy lived like that?) were swept aside. It was then that he introduced me to the word, "*Zwang*." No *Zwang* for him. No butlers. No evening dress.

That was my single glimpse of what he might have been like in Switzerland thirty years before. But he did say something which may have been, though I cannot be sure, more personal. It was much later in the day, and getting dark outside. Einstein was talking about the conditions for a creative existence. He said that, in his experience, the best creative work is never done when one is unhappy. He could scarcely think of any physicist who had done fine work in such a state. Or any composer. Or any writer.

It seemed a strange and unexpected remark.

The only exception he could think of, Einstein went on, was Bohr, who had produced his great paper on the hydrogen spectrum when in deep misery.

Neither Infeld nor I knew that. Einstein was speaking of his famous contemporaries, a generation before our time. I pulled myself together, and suggested Tolstoi when writing *Anna Karenina*. He had been in a state of profound despair. Einstein was interested. Tolstoi was one of his favorite writers. Just as his taste in physics, and his feeling for the nature of the physical laws, was classical, so was his taste in art. He detested romantic art, in particular German romantic art. He didn't like subjectivism. We talked about books. The novel he valued most of all was *The Brothers Karamazov*. Then Einstein came back to his thoughts upon the creative life. His great head was shaking to and fro:

"No, to understand the world one must not be worrying about oneself."

Back in New York, late that night, I found those remarks of his about happiness jumbling with others. At that time I knew little about his own life: I did not know then, and still don't know, whether what he said had any personal relevance. But if it had, it may have been drawn from memories of his own two major creative periods. The first produced the great papers of 1905: he was not long married, his first son was born. I am inclined to fancy that, despite some accounts of those early years, that marriage began by being happy. About his second major period, nearly all the evidence agrees. Despite the war, he was joyous: his cousin Elsa had lifted a burden from him: almost at once he had the transcendental scientific experience of his life.

It was, I think, in that same Long Island house, two years later, that Einstein signed the well-known letter to Roosevelt about the possibility of an atomic bomb. But this event, as I mentioned before, has been wildly melodramatized. Einstein was a mythopoeic character. Some of the myths are true and significant; this myth, though factually true, is not significant.

Let me try to clear the ground. First, Einstein's work had nothing to do either with the discovery or the potential use of nuclear fission. From the moment of the Meitner-Frisch paper in January 1939 (as Niels Bohr said at the time, everyone ought to have seen the meaning of Hahn's 1938 experiments much earlier—"we were all fools"), nuclear fission was a known fact to all physicists in the field. Second, the possible use of nuclear energy had been speculated about long before Einstein produced the equation $E=mc^2$. After the fission experiments, it would have been empirically apparent if there had been no theory at all. Every nuclear physicist in the world—and a good many non-nuclear physicists—were talking about the conceivability of a nuclear bomb from early 1939 onwards. Third, all responsible nuclear physicists wanted to bring this news to their governments as effectively as they could. It happened in England months *before* the Einstein letter was signed. Fourth, a group of refugee scientists in America (Szilard, Wigner, Teller, Fermi) had no direct channels of communication with the White House. Very sensibly, they explained the position to Einstein. It was easy for him to understand. A letter drafted by them, signed by him, handed on by Sachs (an economist with an entrée to the President), would get straight to Roosevelt. "I served as a pillar box," said Einstein. It was signed on Long Island on July 2: it did not reach Roosevelt until October 11. Fifth, if this letter had not been sent, similar messages would have been forced on Roosevelt. For some time *after* the letter, the Americans were much slower off the mark than the English. Peierls's calculations, which showed that the bomb was a possibility, were ready by mid-1940. These had, in historical fact, a major effect upon the *American* scientists. Sixth, in July 1939, there was—unless one was an unqualified pacifist—no moral dilemma. Everyone was afraid that the Nazis would get the bomb first. If so, they would rule the world. It was as simple as that. It was as simple to Einstein as to the crudest of men.

It is a pity that the story of the letter has obscured the genuine moral dilemma of his last years. Which was

—now that the bomb exists, what should a man do? He probably knew little or nothing of the actual development of the bomb. He was not one of the Franck group (once again, organized by Leo Szilard) who protested in advance against its military use on Japan. He was not one, simply because he did not know that the bomb was as good as made. When the first bomb was dropped on Hiroshima, he said simply, "O *weh!*" (Oh horrible!) Nothing would convince him that Hiroshima was forgivable, either in moral or practical terms: just as nothing has convinced many of us, with all the information of the twenty subsequent years, and with our knowledge of how the world has gone.

The bomb was made. What should a man do? He couldn't find an answer which people would listen to. He campaigned for a world state: that only made him distrusted both in the Soviet Union and in the United States. He gave an eschatological warning to a mass television audience in 1950:

And now the public has been advised that the production of the hydrogen bomb is the new goal which will probably be accomplished. An accelerated development towards this end has been solemnly proclaimed by the President. If these efforts should prove successful, radioactive poisoning of the atmosphere, and, hence, annihilation of all life on earth will have been brought within the range of what is technically possible. *A weird aspect of this development lies in its apparently inexorable character. Each step appears as the inevitable consequence of the one that went before.* And at the end, looming ever clearer, lies general annihilation.

That speech made him more distrusted in America. As for practical results, no one listened. Incidentally, in the view of most contemporary military scientists, it would be more difficult totally to eliminate the human species than Einstein then believed. But the most interesting sentences were the ones I have underlined. They are utterly true. The more one has mixed in these horrors, the truer they seem.

He joined in other warnings, one of them signed in the last week of his life. He did not expect them to bite: he retained the hope of his strong spirit, but intellectually he seems to have had no hope at all.

He was physically the strongest of the men I am discussing. He was also the strongest in spirit. He was used to being solitary. "It is strange," he wrote, "to be known so universally and yet to be so lonely." Never mind. He was isolated in his search for the unified field. And the latter was the great theme of his life. He could endure it all, impregnable, and work stoically on. He said: "One must divide one's time between politics and equations. But our equations are much more important to me."

From his late sixties until his death at seventy-six he was continuously ill—from what appear to have been a variety of causes, an intestinal growth, a disease of the liver, finally a weakening of the aorta wall. He lived on in discomfort, and often in acute pain. He stayed cheerful, serene, detached from his own illness and the approach of death. He worked on. The end of his life was neither miserable nor pathetic. "Here on earth I have done my job," he said, without self-pity.

By his bedside, one Sunday night, lay some pages of manuscript. They included more equations leading to the unified field theory, which he had never found. He hoped to be enough out of pain next day to work on them. Early in the morning the aortic blister broke, and he died.

Good, gentle, wise, Hardy called him, that day at Fenner's. At the time I wanted to add another word. If we were having the conversation again, I think I should have chosen a clumsy one. Of all the men I have heard of, this one was—in any sense I can imagine, intellectual, emotional, spiritual—the most unbudgeable.

LLOYD GEORGE

I met Lloyd George by sheer accident, and the actual manner of it sounds more improbable than anyone would be prepared to invent. I had gone to Antibes for the Christmas of 1937 and was staying at the Hotel du Cap waiting for a friend to join me. There, in the same hotel, was Lloyd George, in the middle of a family party. I used to watch him taking a morning stroll through the grounds to Eden Roc; his hair streamed in the breeze, his cloak swung with his lively step, he walked like a strong and active man in middle-age (he was seventy-three). I watched him also in the dining-room. His party had a table, the star table, in the window corner. The room was large and lofty, and there were very few people in it that Christmas; Lloyd George's laughter filled it. From an obscure place beside the opposite wall, I watched him curiously, thinking of all I had heard and read about him.

On the afternoon of Christmas Day I went for a long walk. I was lonely: it was a time in my life when most things were going wrong. As the sun went down, I remember that it was a bright cold Mediterranean winter evening, with frost glinting blue under the cornice lights.

When I got back to the hotel, the porter called me: there was a message from Major Gwilym Lloyd George. Would I ring him up? As soon as possible? From the porter's desk I did so. Major Gwilym was saying amiably that his father had noticed that I was alone. Would I care to join their party that night? I was delighted. I was also, as I got ready for dinner, distinctly perplexed. Why ever should this happen? I was a completely unknown young man. Had they mistaken me for someone else?

No, when I arrived down for dinner, Lloyd George greeted me by name, welcoming me as though he had wanted to meet me for years. I said (and meant it) that I was honored. He asked me questions, and I asked some back. It was all easy. He was not a self-conscious man, and nor was I.

But none of that explained why I had been invited. It might have been Christmas charity, it crossed my mind, or even a habit of his: much later Major Gwilym, who had then become Lord Tenby, told me that he had never known his father to do such a thing before. In fact, it was not long after that first meeting that I had unearthed the truth. It turned out to be simple, slightly comic, and not specially flattering to me. When I knew him a little better, I asked him directly why he had picked me out: it was great good luck for me, but why had he done it? He was too good-mannered not to look slightly sheepish. But we were close enough now and I prodded him. "Well, as a matter of fact," he said, "I thought you had an interesting head."

He had, I found, a passion for phrenology. His intuitive judgment of men was of the highest class and like others of his kind, like one or two great industrialists that I met later, he wanted a pseudo-scientific framework for his skill. I had been selected as a subject for cranial investigation.

That did not matter. As we ate our Christmas dinner, he went out of his way to make me happy, and the rest of the party, and incidentally himself. I had been prepared for his charm, but I ought to have known that charm of his quality (which is often the cause of moral reprobation in those who do not possess it) is not simply a trick that one switches on for a purpose. Naturally he often used it for a purpose: he was a professional politician, selfish and ruthless, in love with power. But he was also engaged by human beings: he was capable of a detached and humorous interest; he might be selfish but he wanted to please; he was not self-involved: at times—in a way quite impossible for more sanctimonious men—he could forget himself. As a result he set one talking and listened, not as a political trick (though it had become first nature to use it as a political trick) but because he liked doing so.

This was one of the roots of his charm. Lord Hankey, who had been Secretary of his Cabinet and who loved and admired him—this was stranger than it seems since Hankey, beneath a mild and simple façade, was not over-given either to love or admiration—once told me during the second war:—the difference between L.G. and Winston is this. Imagine the subject of balloons crops up. Winston, without a blink will give you a brilliant hour-long lecture on balloons. L.G., even if he has never seen you before, will spend an hour finding out anything you know or think about them.

At that Christmas dinner, his eyes flashed and sparkled. They were a deep blue: in any party they did not leave a single person unnoticed. I kept finding them upon me. They were mischievous, they were clairvoyant, they were often lit up with dashing malice. They were the eyes of one aware, without strain or effort, of any shade of feeling round him.

I had several surprises at that first meeting. I had somehow expected him to be a teetotaller. I was relieved to find that this was not so. In fact he took a manifest pleasure in choosing the wine. I had not imagined that he was an excellent mimic, or that he was ready to use this talent in recalling historical scenes in which he had taken part. It struck me as odd, though gratifying, to hear the proceedings of the Big Four at Versailles mimicked, in extreme high spirits, by one of them. He was the least pompous of men. He gave me that turn before I had known him a couple of hours.

I was also surprised, though in a different fashion, by his taste in reading. History? Yes, of all kinds. (Politicians usually read history with the pleasant anticipation that posterity will read similarly of them. Just as great scientists—this was pre-eminently true of Rutherford—felt that the history of science is a study deserving all possible encouragement.) Fiction? No, not much. Why not? It made him too sad. This seemed to me so bizarre that I probed a little further. After all, no one had ever accused L.G. of a lack of realism in action, or of not taking a robustly practical view of life and his fellow men. Most serious novels had sad endings, he explained. He did not like being depressed. So, before he read a novel, he enquired what its ending was like. If it was unhappy he could not bear to read it.

That was that. It made me feel unlucky in my vocation. Particularly as L.G. blithely assured me that he took a Wild West story to bed with him every night of his life.

He did so, that Christmas night. Also the remainder of a bottle of champagne. He sang a song in Welsh, and then went upstairs two at a time. It was well before ten, but later than his usual hour for bed. He liked, so he told me, to be in bed by half-past nine, read his Wild West story for twenty minutes, turn off the lights and sleep at once and without a break till six. That was his habit. He had been kept awake by a public care only once in his career. I wish I had asked him when it was, but at a first meeting I had not quite the nerve. The U-boats in 1917? The March offensive in 1918? I had a suspicion that it might have been the political coup in 1916.

Anyway, phrenologically or otherwise, I was in favor. I was to join his table so long as I was free, he said. So I had days of his company; and at Easter went back to Antibes, where he was still staying, and talked to him night after night.

I must not pretend to an intimacy greater than I possessed. Like many men of immediate spontaneity, he was also deeply cagey; some things, like politics, he would talk to me nakedly about, some things not at all. On my side, I hadn't much to give him. Novels he didn't care about, and science less. As for dons (I was one at the time) his approval of them was distinctly luke-warm. "Who have you got at Cambridge?" he once asked me: crassly, I mentioned the name of Keynes, noticed an unusually flashing eye, and went on in a hurry to pick up the brick: Keynes had once told me, I said, that L.G. was one of the only two politicians he had known who was clever enough to be a first-class academician. This story was entirely true: Keynes was as unfair to politicians as L.G. was to dons. L.G. was slightly mollified. But then old wounds gave twinges: the economic consequences of the Peace, donnish gibes, may have come back to memory (he didn't like criticism more than any other man). "Keynes!" he cried. "Keynes used to put his head round the door of my room during the war, and say our finances wouldn't last another fortnight." Keynes was accordingly, so L.G. said, ordered out of the room, not once but often. I have no idea what substance there was in this anecdote; but at least it indicated that Cambridge dons were not, by virtue of their office, popular. Still he did not hold my job against me.

Much of the talk was somber. World politics were dark, war was coming: more than once he said, "I have no comfort to give you." Yet his spirits were so high, his absence of self-pity so complete, that it was great fun. Even though there was a generation and a half between us (by a comic fluke, in years to come my son sat in the same form in the same school as his *great-grandson*), even though our codes of manners belonged to different epochs. I never once heard anyone call him by his Christian name: I believe that only Winston Churchill did so: L.G. strongly objected—with a stiffness odd, one would have thought, for his temperament, and a little old-fashioned even in Edwardian England—to others doing so. So far as he needed a form of address in conversation, which wasn't often, he used my surname: so far as I needed a form of address, which also wasn't often, I called him "sir."

A contrast struck me a quarter of a century later, when someone else I knew became Prime Minister—Harold Wilson, who reminded me more of L.G. than any politician I had met. Forty-eight hours after the election (in October 1964) I was summoned to Number 10. Harold Wilson was sitting alone in the Cabinet Room, in the place in the middle of the long table where his predecessors had sat. I said: "Good evening, Prime Minister." A slow, steady, unpretending puma-like grin faced me. "It used to be Harold," he said.

As I say, the resemblance between the two men had often struck me, and was to do so more and more: but L.G. could never have behaved like that.

Yet L.G. was a radical to his bones, and in a profound sense his radicalism never left him. It is now common form to say that L.G. was the better politician, Churchill the greater statesman. There I confess my own predilections make me have my doubts. It would be perverse not to agree that Churchill had the more rigid and upright character: but I should have thought that it was equally perverse not to agree that L.G. had by far the deeper social insight. A progressive-minded man will blind himself to some of L.G.'s faults: a romantic, magnanimous reactionary will do the same for Churchill. It is pleasant to think, though, that they were close friends through all the turbulence of their careers, right up to L.G.'s death.

Lloyd George ⋈ 129

L.G. seems to have been (as Lady Asquith of Yarnbury fairly but disapprovingly reports) the only political figure in the country whom Churchill regarded with veneration. For years he was Churchill's teacher. In return, Churchill saved him in the Marconi scandal, which might have been political ruin. When L.G. became Prime Minister, he took a comparable risk and paid that debt in full.

Often they were allies, two of the toughest allies who can ever have worked together in politics: often they were closer than allies, in a game where friendship doesn't enter much. Towards the end, when Churchill came to power and L.G. was old, ill, and alienated from the war, Churchill still tried to bring him back to public life. It brought a gleam of pleasure into those pathetic last years: "The Prime Minister has made me honorable offers," L.G. liked to say.

When I was talking to him, a little earlier, and he was still in full vigor, he often spoke of Churchill. He spoke always in the same tone. It was a tone curiously mixed of affection, quasi-respect, and a kind of mockery. He admired Churchill's strength, his power, his inventiveness, his undefeatable intransigence—but, with a kind of Welsh malice (which often made me feel that he was looking at Englishmen through a foreigner's eyes), he thought him a bit of an ass. "The trouble with Winston," (I don't think that my memory is playing me tricks: I am almost sure that he usually referred to Churchill by his Christian name) he said, "is that he's always taking action. He *will insist on getting out his maps*. In 1914 he got out his map of the Dardanelles, and think where that landed us. And after the war I had to think what to do with him. I wanted him in my Cabinet, of course: but what's the safest place *after a war* for a man who will get out his maps? Minister of War, of course, I thought. He'll be safe there. But was he? Before I could look round, he'd got out his maps of Russia and we were making fools of ourselves in the Civil War. [He was not given to regrets about the actions of his governments, but this was one that he came back to.] When that was over, he got out his maps again. This time he got out his maps of Greece and Turkey, and that brought my tottering administration to a close."

I cannot vouch for every word of that speech, of course, but it is near enough. A good many of the phrases have stuck in my mind. It was unfair: after all, he had been Prime Minister: but it was not meaningless.

Well, there they are, the two of them, preserved in time, the great conservative, the great irregular radical.

It was partly an accident of birth that gave a singular quality to L.G.'s radicalism. He was born Welsh and he spoke Welsh: as I have indicated, he saw England and the English class structure as a foreigner sees it. He never liked it, any more than his friend Beaverbrook, another foreigner, liked it. He chose never to be inside. He became one of the kings of this world: but there lurked within him the resentment of his upbringing, of a poor people outside the fringe, of a despised culture, of the Chapel against the Established Church.

That may have been a political advantage: it was easier for him, all through his life, to identify himself with the poor and put-upon than it has usually been for Englishmen, even those born as humbly as he was. But he also had what may have been a disadvantage: he was brought up in agricultural Wales, in as near an approach to a peasant society as this island had preserved. This reinforced a strain of his radicalism; he knew, in his flesh and bone, what an agricultural laborer feels towards a landowner. But it also set him at an angle from the emerging new radicalism of his time—which otherwise he was superabundantly equipped to understand, mold and use. For years, right up to 1914, he was the only powerful politician with a voice that went deep into the population: but after 1918, with the rise of the Labor Party, such a voice could only have full resonance if it spoke to and for the industrial working class. That L.G. could not do. His radicalism was passionate but not all of a piece, made up of prophetic insights about the Welfare State (in founding which he made his greatest feat of statecraft) blended with relics of small-country nationalism together with the furious anti-gamekeeper, pro-teetotal, nonconformist cries of rural Wales. Not that he was a teetotaller, as I have said before: nor a believing noncomformist. He was one of the cleverest of men: he had deep social insight: but his social passions never got organized into an intellectual framework. It is worthwhile comparing him with Lenin, born five years later, the only contemporary of his with greater political gifts.

Still, from the time he entered Parliament in 1890—as an obscure Welsh attorney—to the beginning of the war, he was the effective spokesman of the country's left. Both in opposition and in government he used this position with consummate political skill. He fought his contemporary battles—against the Boer War, against the Conservative Education Bill of 1902—just as in 1966 he would have been fighting against the Vietnamese war and educational segregation. And he performed out of comparison more powerfully than any of his latter-day successors. He was, it is clear, a supreme orator: better on the platform than in the Commons, although Harold Macmillan has told me that some of his parliamentary speeches were the best he has ever heard.

Here perhaps one ought to say that oratory, like humorous art, doesn't wear well: the styles change too fast. When I was about seventeen, I heard him speak at the old Leicester Drill Hall. I remember being disappointed, not so much with the content as with the manner: it already seemed high-flown and old-fashioned. In just the same way, I doubt if Churchill's great war-time speeches would be acceptable today. The rate of change in oratory has been increasing, and television has made it faster still. A quite new style of parliamentary speaking has grown up: more subdued, more conversational, a good deal less theatrical. The rhetoric is still there, because all speaking contains its stratum of rhetoric, but it is much more carefully subdued. Of course, if L.G. were a young man today, he would master this new version of the art, and television also: all the evidence suggests that no one ever had more natural ability in the oral skills. But it is no use reading his old speeches, or anyone else's old speeches, in the hope of capturing their effect. One has to rely on the judgment of those present, who were attuned to them.

As soon as he got into the Cabinet, in the Liberal Government of 1906, he showed the full range of his gifts. He had been a great tribune, but he was also a great minister. He had the extreme advantage of believing in what he was doing: that is, he believed, with all the rancor of past poverty, with the fellow-feeling for the unprivileged that he never quite forgot, in what we should now call the Welfare State. Rather strangely, he had picked up his first administrative ideas in Prussia; as Chancellor of the Exchequer, he forced them through. To the end of his life, this was the achievement he liked to talk of.

Further, he was after power, the real power, the top place. He wouldn't have been in politics if he hadn't wanted the power, nor would anyone else of his quality. He knew that he was in a tricky, but ultimately strong tactical position. The government—incidentally, a very gifted one, though still oligarchic—was mildly, very mildly, reformist. He stood on its extreme left. To the left in the country, just beginning to murmur, he was the one guarantee of hope. A powerful politician in such a government, on the left of his Cabinet colleagues, known to be on the left, is going to attract maximum hatred. But he also had two sources of strength. L.G. knew this, both by instinct and calculation. He told me so thirty years later. He may have been rationalizing a little, but I think it was not all hindsight.

The first advantage is obvious enough: unlike his colleagues he had an extra source of support, he could strike responses outside Parliament, outside conventional politics, in what L.G. himself would have called "the country." The second advantage is more subtle. I believe I gathered what he meant, but I am putting it in a more modern idiom. In any reformist government a certain number of its members would half-like to be more on the left than they actually are. That appears to have been true of some of L.G.'s colleagues. He stood for causes which made them feel guilty. He acquired the moral initiative. It is significant—though L.G. did not say this—that Churchill, not an impressionable character, in no conceivable sense a man of the left, became full of respect for L.G.'s social insights, and for years followed his lead.

In this position, as I have just said, he was bound to attract maximum hatred. Conservative society is quick to spot its most dangerous enemy and on the whole fairly shrewd about identifying him. For many years in conservative circles L.G. was the most hated man in England —much as in similar American circles Franklin Roosevelt was the most hated man in the United States. In some enclaves this hatred lasted long after L.G.'s war-time administration. During one of my stays at Antibes, an elderly country gentleman, rich, titled, decent, obtuse, came to pay a visit to the hotel. I happened to have met him, and I mentioned that L.G. was walking in the grounds. The old gentleman shuddered, and said he must get out of the way. "I couldn't possibly shake hands," he remarked desperately, "with a man that I detest." I left him waiting for his hosts, and a few minutes later ran into L.G., to whom I passed the word. Half-an-hour later I reappeared, and found a small party having tea—a married couple, the old gentleman and L.G. L.G.'s charm was effervescing, the old gentleman looked stupefied and pleased.

The hatred had been accumulating since he entered the Commons, long before he was in office, although it was its most intense between 1906 and 1914. It was, at its root, political hatred, but he gave his enemies some extra-political excuses to hang on to. The most genuine of the excuses was the Marconi scandal in 1912, where he behaved with a folly which even now it is hard to understand. The story is well known. The Cabinet had knowledge that a government contract was to be placed with the English Marconi Company; the managing director of this company was Godfrey Isaacs, the brother of Sir Rufus Isaacs (later Lord Reading), the Attorney-General. Rumors went round that Rufus Isaacs, Lloyd George and the Chief Whip of the government party had, on the strength of this inside knowledge, been speculating in the company's shares. The rumors were formally denied, in the House of Commons, by Sir Rufus Isaacs. This denial was factually accurate. But no one thought it worth while saying that Rufus Isaacs had bought ten thousand shares of the new issue of the firm's American subsidiary, and had sold one thousand to the other two. These transactions were made openly, without any attempt at concealment. It was such an imbecile thing to do that all concerned must have been innocent. But it nearly ejected L.G. out of politics for good. For, as anyone but a future Lord Chief Justice might have divined, the story duly came out. Partisan feeling was acute, and the conservatives handled their attack clumsily, on plain party lines; if they had been more judicious, it would have been harder for L. G. to survive. As it was, he had to rely on the absolute fighting loyalty of Winston Churchill, one of the better allies in this kind of corner: and on the calm Olympian support of Asquith, who might, if he had been a less magnanimous man, have disinterested himself and so, passively and without effort, have got rid of his most dangerous rival.

It is a not displeasing coda to the story that, when the accounts for the whole transaction were toted up, all three men turned out to have lost money.

The Marconi affair was one gibe against L.G. The other, less dangerous but longer lasting, was women. Early in his career he had been mentioned in a divorce case: a woman signed a confession that on February 4, 1896, at her home in Montgomeryshire, she committed adultery with Lloyd George, M.P. L.G. produced to Counsel the parliamentary division lists, which showed that on February 4 he had been voting in the Commons lobby until the early morning. Well, that was that. But, through much of his career, similar charges kept recurring. Baldwin and other Tories called him "the Goat." Since his death there have been accounts of a life of extravagant womanizing.

There is no need to regard those accounts as the concrete truth. Nevertheless, L.G. was fond of women. Many eminent politicians, of whom Churchill was one, have no use even for women's company: with L.G. the opposite was true. For me at least this softened him, made him more complicated and more likeable. And it was easy to imagine that, to many women, particularly to intelligent women, he had been one of the most attractive of men. For weeks I saw Frances Stevenson near to him. In 1911, when he was Chancellor, she became his secretary at the age of twenty-three. She has described her first meeting, when he interviewed her for the job.

I recall the sensitive face, with deep furrows between the eyes: the eyes themselves, in which was all knowledge of human nature, grave and gay almost simultaneously: eyes which, when they scrutinized you, convinced you that they understood all the workings of your heart and mind, sympathized with all your difficulties, set you in a place apart. The broad brow; the beautiful profile—straight nose, neat resolute chin. And a complexion as young and fresh as a child's. But there was something more even than this which distinguished him from all other men I had ever met—from all men whom I ever did meet thereafter —a magnetism which made my heart leap and swept aside my judgment.

A man would be hard to please if he wanted more than that—from an exceptionally clever and charming young woman. From that day she devoted her life to him. After his first wife died, when he was near his own death, he married her.

It has sometimes occurred to me that Edwardian politicians were a lot more careless or reckless than their successors. Several of the great Edwardians, for instance, were obsessive drinkers (not L.G., who was temperate in that respect) : if a modern top politician drank as much, he would not stand the pace long. And, of that same group, it was not only L.G. who loved women, though there was a spectrum of shades of commitment. Asquith's relation with Venetia Stanley was clearly innocent: and yet fifty years later, we should be inclined to cast a bleak eye on a Prime Minister who sat through Cabinet meetings writing love-letters. Politicians can get divorced without ruin nowadays, but they have become more disciplined. Most of all they have become more disciplined in their financial behavior. Whatever the rights and wrongs of the case, anyone behaving as Rufus Isaacs, L.G. and the Chief Whip behaved over the Marconi shares would be out of politics without a question asked. No one would even bother about the rights and wrongs: the man would be out, and irretrievably out. No modern minister would dare to have dealings in any business where government was remotely concerned: or, if he is prudent, any speculative dealings at all. He would not even let his wife go shopping in an official car. In all these ways we have become financially puritanical to the limit. It may seem finicky, but I am sure that it is an unmitigated gain.

In very much the same fashion, the group of military leaders whom L.G. had to use, when he seized the power in 1916, were remarkably—and almost disastrously—less disciplined than Churchill's a quarter of a century later. It is easy to say, from the viewpoint of our different society, that L.G. ought to have avoided Paschendale and, if necessary, sacked Haig: if L.G. had done so, he would have been got rid of himself. As he used to say, they all made every imaginable error: and finally won the war. And he had seized the power both for its own sake and—politicians have to be given credit for what they aim at—to do just that.

The details of the intrigue which ousted Asquith are now well known: Beaverbrook's is the most vivid account of any coup in high-level politics, written by the supreme middle-man, the secret operator—and in the end the fall guy. Once he had served his purpose he too was thrown out: and his rueful, sardonic observation of his own fate is the best part of the story. For a more objective version one

Lloyd George ❋ 139

has to read Roy Jenkins's biography of Asquith. It is not desirable to be over-subtle about L.G.'s part in arriving in the top place. One night Hankey—who saw it all happening—was asked why L.G. found it necessary to become Prime Minister. Hankey had two voices: one was that of the trained and super-discreet Cabinet Secretary, muted, Polonius-like. In that he answered, "Because of the consciousness of his great powers." Hankey's second voice, which he kept for privileged occasions, was simple and down-to-earth. In that he answered: "Because he wanted the job." Both comments were true.

Hankey said something else. He was the last man to indulge in hero-worship: he was the one person in high places throughout 1914–18 who had a professional knowledge of war: about war, and the influence of personalities upon it, he took a severely Tolstoyan attitude. Yet he said that, if L.G. had not become Prime Minister, he did not believe that the war could have been won.

No one doubts that L.G. and Churchill are the greatest War Ministers this country has thrown up. I have heard arguments as to which was the greater: but those arguments don't seem to me to have much meaning. The circumstances of the two wars, the part that this country played in them, were radically different. In the first war this country was the senior partner. In fact one can draw a not too far-fetched comparison between the roles of L.G. and Clemenceau in that war, and those of Roosevelt and Churchill in the second. L.G. and Roosevelt are in many respects comparable figures: irregular, radical reformers in peace-time, hated by the right wing, made to transform themselves into war-leaders. Neither had any detailed military knowledge: both had excellent strategic judgment. On the other side, Churchill and Clemenceau, the junior partners, were the incarnation of conservative nationalist patriotic will. Between L.G. and Roosevelt, at any rate, some of the political and psychological resemblances seem to go deeper.

I am going to allow myself a chauvinistic aside. In the first war, as I say, this country was the senior partner. We were much richer than the French. We produced most of the munitions and, by the end, the larger number of fighting troops. The French took, both absolutely and in proportion to the population, the heavier casualties. Therefore it would have been intolerable for the French not to have a Frenchman as supreme commander. In the second war, the United States was the senior partner. They were much richer than the British. They produced most of the munitions, and, by the end, the larger number of fighting troops. The British took, both absolutely and in proportion to the population, the heavier casualties. Therefore it would have been intolerable for the Americans not to have an American as supreme commander. In precisely what circumstances would an Englishman have got the top job?

Neither L.G. nor Roosevelt had any detailed military knowledge. Churchill had a great deal. It is arguable which is the better equipment for the supreme political leader in times of war. Of the political leaders in the 1939–45 war, only Churchill, Hitler and perhaps Stalin (who seems to have had first-class military judgment) took a detailed interest, not only in strategy, but in tactics and weapons. In Hitler's case, he was often wiser than his soldiers; but when he went wrong, he went catastrophically wrong. As for the Anglo-American side, the thorough critical examination has yet to be made. At this distance it looks as though the curious equipoise between Roosevelt listening to his military, and Churchill talking actively to his, worked, within the human limits, very well: better than the ramshackle arrangements of 1914–18, which happened, we must remember, when only a few oddities like Hankey had the faintest conception of the meaning of total war.

L.G. had none of Churchill's passion for the military art: but his mind—despite, or perhaps because of, his leaps of imagination—was level, critical and quantitative. When I was talking to him, he was engaged heart and soul in the Spanish Civil War: this was the last radical cause of his life: nevertheless, on the military events his judgment stayed detached. I was involved myself, at least as much as he was. Morning after morning we studied the news. Even after Teruel, he would not let me have false hopes. He could not see how the Russian aid to the government could balance the German aid to Franco: the puzzle was, what the Germans and Russians were playing for.

Sometimes, from a private intelligence service which he maintained, he received his own information. By the spring of 1938 it was uncomfortable to hear. Yet, still buoyant, he would cheer me up with gibes about military communiqués. The main principle in reading them, so L.G. said, was to remember that it is difficult to lie when one knows *for certain* the unpleasant truth. That is, a military headquarters will not normally claim a town it is nowhere near: nor thousands of prisoners, if it has captured none. But when it has nothing to go on, as in "losses inflicted on the enemy," or "aircraft brought down in the sea," or "damage inflicted by bombing," it will lie with the utmost enthusiasm. "Look for the prisoners! Look for places! Pay no attention to the rest!" L.G. exhorted me. I found this instruction valuable, though at times discouraging, between 1939 and 1945.

Soon after I met him he told me that he had received an invitation from the Spanish government: would he take up office in Barcelona and become a kind of super-Minister of Supply? He told us this more as though he had still not made up his mind: we even discussed whom we might recruit, if he said yes. But reluctantly, I knew it was a day-dream. Perhaps he was older than he seemed: certainly he was too realistic to fling himself into something like chaos, from which there was no chance of emerging on the winning side. He did not want a messy failure. I did not know then, and have not discovered since, the details of the invitation. It is not mentioned in anything written about him. But my memory is quite clear. He may have been embroidering somewhat, but with me he discussed the proposition as I have just recorded. And I wished then, and went on wishing later—I admit romantically—that he had gone. It would have been a better end than the one that he was fated to make.

Of course, he could not have gone. The whole habit and passion of a lifetime prevented it. He was totally involved—while with masterly military detachment he instructed me about the Spanish war—with the chessboard of English politics. Even then: in his seventies:

Lloyd George ✻ 143

when there was no realistic chance of his ever ruling again. He could not repress the springs of hope. I remember the result of a by-election coming through, and L.G. was overjoyed. "I hear the government are taking it very seriously," he said. He was radiant with malicious pleasure at Chamberlain's expense: L.G. despised him more than any man alive ("a narrow thin mean skull! a narrow thin mean man!").

He was radiant not only with malicious pleasure, for there were calculations running through his mind. There might still be a swing. There could be sudden changes, even in parliamentary democracies: a move here, a move there, it was a long chance, but it might still come off. There was still the faintest flicker of a hope. For days the result of that by-election was more vivid to him than anything in the world. I thought that the pursuit of power could be a passion more preoccupying and more irresistible than passions of the flesh. But at that time intellectual persons, having ceased to be prudish about sex, had become idiotically prudish about power. This passion, at its most grandiose, got linked more closely than the sexual passion to a kind of supreme vanity. That was true of L.G. For he, the most subtle and proficient of flatterers, himself constantly required flattery. Like Rutherford he was vain on the grand scale.

This specific flaw was partly responsible for the trouble he had got into the year before I met him, and which hag-rode him for the rest of his life. In 1936 he went to Berchtesgaden to meet Hitler. We know more about Hitler than we did then: in the circles in which I moved, we had judged his dangerousness accurately enough, but we did not realize that he was a man of evil genius: we were inclined to think that face-to-face he would be slightly comic. It is clear that he was not in the least comic: he could be terrifying, even to very tough men (Molotov, the toughest of the tough, seems to have been one of the few who were quite unmoved): he could also, when he cared, exercise great charm. At this Berchtesgaden meeting, he both out-charmed and out-flattered L.G. There is no doubt that L.G. came away admiring and bemused.

It was, however, not only Hitler's flattery which made him willing to admire. He was, as I have said, an irregular radical all through his life, but had never found an intellectual form for his politics. Churchill, for instance, had a rigid and pious reverence for the parliamentary process. This might be old-fashioned, but it gave him an honorable base. L.G. had no such reverence: and he had escaped the influences which trade unionists or ordinary left wingers were brought up under, which, whatever their faults, gave them a steady insight into what National-Socialism really meant. L.G. in his anarchic, rebellious way searched for those parts of it which had a radical tinge: and he could find some.

The saddening result was that he felt ambivalent about Germany until the war began, and for some time afterwards. He was firm, and more than firm, over Spain: he was firm about Italian Fascism, which he detested: he was firm about getting rid of Chamberlain in 1940, when he made the last of his great Commons speeches. But, though sometimes he made it seem otherwise, he would not take an official part in the war. True, he was old, but Churchill and Beaverbrook, loyal as ever, went right beyond the edge of duty to bring him in. Partly, perhaps, to recall the glory of the first war: but much more because Churchill wanted his gifts, calculating that doubts would disappear, fire would burn up again, because he was in action. That might have turned out true: but L.G. would not come in. He liked being asked: he gave various excuses for saying no, among them the valid one that he would face, in Chamberlain, implacable hostility in the War Cabinet. In secret, he never meant to join.

As he grew older he was the victim of his own realism. In 1940 he could see no prospect of winning the war. He had affection for Churchill, but not the respect that Churchill had for him. He believed that the government would be discredited. It is possible—this is a guess for which I have no evidence—he still thought that, when the government was discredited, he would be called back to power at last.

In 1941, before Russia was brought into the war, he said in Parliament that he could see no end to the war and no hope. At that time there was no realistic hope. But, if it had been the first war, he would have subdued his realism. In the spring of 1941 one did not need realism. It would have been the worst of guides: that is why the country was lucky to have Churchill.

Then, at last, when Russia and the United States were fighting, L.G. had become too old to care much. Soon afterwards he was diagnosed as having cancer, though he was not told. Just once, on the day of the invasion of France, his old spirit flared up, and he went to the House of Commons, happy about the war after all his doubts, to congratulate his old and stubborn friend.

Those last years were sad. Yet he could forget—as I often heard him forget—the chess-board of power and his own contrivances past and present. He could talk about the world history of his own time and about the future with a beautiful detachment. I have always remembered one night in the great drawing room of the Antibes hotel. It was a tremendous room, brilliant with light, the curtains left undrawn: down below, beyond the grounds, beyond Eden Roc, we could hear the sea, thudding, sucking. We were alone. L.G. was talking of his place in history. Of how he would be regarded mainly as one of those who tried to soften the class-struggle. And people who wanted the class-struggle naked would come down against him, and others would be for. He would get some attention for his part in the Great War—the 1914–18 war (this conversation took place in 1938). But nothing of that counted much, L.G. was saying, against the great movements in history. None of our struggles mattered much, wars or revolutions or what you will, as compared with the sheer biological and geographical facts. Whatever happened, in two hundred years, perhaps sooner, the balance of the world would have changed. The industrialization of Russia was taking place: India would follow: perhaps China, in a hundred years. (Note the time-scale, and the precedence of India over China. He would certainly, if speaking now, shorten the first and change the second.) Whatever governments presided over the operations, these changes would make our local concerns look no more significant than the Wars of the Roses.

WINSTON CHURCHILL

LIKE most people of my age, I remember—I shall not forget it while I live—the beautiful, cloudless, desperate summer of 1940. One night I was listening with a friend, for we were never far from a radio that June, to one of the grand Churchillian speeches. The accent was odd, to our more modern English ears. It was nothing liked the clipped upper-class English which was already fashionable and was to become more so. The style of oratory, like that of Lloyd George, was obsolescent. But we noticed neither of those things as we listened that night, and other summer nights. For that voice was our hope. It was the voice of will and strength incarnate. It was saying what we wanted to hear said ("We shall never surrender") and what we tried to believe, sometimes against the protests of realism and common sense, would come true. ("We shall fight on unconquerable until the curse of Hitler is lifted from the brows of mankind. We are sure that in the end all will come right.")

My friend and I listened, and when the speech was

over went out into the London summer evening. He said: "We must never deny our gratitude. Don't forget. We must *never* deny our gratitude."

Oddly enough, most of us were very happy in those days. There was a kind of collective euphoria over the whole country. I don't know what we were thinking about. We were very busy. We had a purpose. We were living in constant excitement, usually, if we examined the true position, of an unpromising kind. In one's realistic moments, it was difficult to see what chance we had. But I doubt if most of us had many realistic moments, or thought much at all. We were working like mad. We were sustained by a surge of national emotion, of which Churchill was both symbol and essence, evocator and voice.

The English (I can't bring myself to use the American word "British," but the Scotch and Welsh can overlook the sub-divisions) are a deeply nationalistic people, as much so as any in the world. Despite the class structure, they are, or at least they were in 1940, capable of feeling as one nation. Compare the behavior of the French and English rich at the start of the second war—better Hitler than our socialists, we heard from some prosperous acquaintances in Paris. The English rich did not say that or behave like that when it came to the point. Those who might have been tempted (there were some) couldn't live it out, in the face of Churchill and the forces that he spoke for.

There were some who were tempted otherwise. Of course there were. Each of us knew people who were not to be trusted if the test came. One mustn't romanticize:

the collective behavior was better than the suspicious had ever dared to hope, but there were people who, under the pressures which occupied Europe suffered, would, through class interest, political interest or, much more, stark self-preservation, have taught us the meaning of the word collaborator. We shall never know how many. At the time, we did not worry. The idiom of conversation took on a curious, jaunty air, as though patriotism could only be assumed if one was sarcastic about it. I was sitting in an air raid shelter that September with a senior civil servant: we were discussing the theoretical plans for evacuating governmental departments. In the case of my own, this was academic, since we had to operate in London or cease to operate at all. In the case of his, the department might feasibly be moved. "It will not, however, happen," he said, in a precise, old-fashioned, mandarin tone. "The Prime Minister has determined that we shall die in the last ditch: and there is no one inclined to say him nay."

Churchill's patriotism was, of course, absolute. It took in the whole of his nature. He was an aristocrat, but he would cheerfully have beggared his class and his friends, and everyone else too, if that was the price of the country coming through. We believed it of him. The poor believed it, as his voice rolled out in to the slum streets, those summer evenings of 1940. The national emotion stayed at that pitch for some months, if anything heightened by the air raids. I think it was flagging before a year had passed, probably by the spring of 1941. But during this period Churchill spoke for a nation undivided and curiously happy, as it has never been in my lifetime, before or since.

Winston Churchill ※

Looking back, perhaps one reads into our mood of these months elements which were not there. Did we really have a sense of last things, as I have now? The last fight of Britain as a solitary great power (I think we had intimations that, whatever happened, we should not after this be, in the full sense, a great power again). The last great starring part on the world stage. The last aristocrat to rule—not preside over, rule—the country. The last assertive cry of a nation which, for no particular reason, had governed a disproportionate slice of the world.

All these things, and a good many more, seem now to be contained in Churchill's speeches. Nowadays I think about them in two ways. If I am depressed about England, then they sharpen the resemblance to the Republic of Venice, another great conquering state, for a thousand years important out of proportion to its resources. In their twilight they suddenly threw up a tremendous fighting Doge, Francesco Morosini, who went off, summoned up the whole of Venetian history, and in person led his troops to conquer the Peloponnese—which Churchill would have been entirely capable of doing (incidentally, Morosini made a nearly fatal dent in the sinking Venetian economy: Churchill would have been capable of that too). If I am depressed about our society, then I am sometimes afraid that the first half of the Hitler war was our last great collective effort in the twilight. If I am feeling cheerful about our future, then I fancy that, in a different and socially better Britain, our descendants will think of it with at least a sneaking pride. Macaulay said of Oliver Cromwell that everyone, whether they believed in kings or not, could not help feeling that he was the greatest prince who ever ruled in England. I suspect that may be something like the attitude of posterity to Churchill, at any rate in the first year of his war-time administration.

Yet there are paradoxes which will puzzle posterity, if in fact they are interested in this period at all. During that year, and to a less extent during much of the war, Churchill *ruled* the country more comprehensively, more directly, and with a greater measure of support, than any Prime Minister has ever done. Nevertheless, he became Prime Minister only against the ill-will of the overwhelming majority of his own party. When Chamberlain had to go, they would have chosen Lord Halifax as Prime Minister. King George VI, who represented decent conservative opinion very well, thought Halifax "the obvious man," and hated having to send for Churchill.

This was in May 1940, with the Germans driving into France. It looks as though Churchill would never have been sent for, if it had not been for the absurd but providential chance that Halifax happened to be a member of the House of Lords. When Churchill as Prime Minister was making his first speeches in the Commons, he got very little applause from his own party. His real support came from the labor benches opposite.

Then there was another twist. He was Prime Minister for five years. The Hitler war was won. There was a general election. He was promptly thrown out of office— "dismissed" to use his own word—by a gigantic labor majority, in the biggest political turnover in English history.

These events are calculated to puzzle, not only posterity, but also contemporary Americans. Many visiting Englishmen have been asked about them in the United States. There are various levels of explanation, including two, which, true as far as they go, do not go far enough. First, the magic (or mana or charisma or whatever is the current sociological term) of a British Prime Minister is always less with us than the magic of an American president in the U.S.A. This is because the magical component of authority in Britain is taken away from those who have the power and invested in the monarch. There is still a residue of veneration for the monarch, which is, in an anthropological sense, magical, and none to spare for the Prime Minister, however wonderful he may be.

Second, and this is a banal truth which ought not to be forgotten in Anglo-American exchanges, everything looks greener the other side of the hill. Franklin Roosevelt was worshipped in England to an extent which many Americans to this day find it hard to believe. In a foreign country, all the political battles of the past, all the grudges and feuds, are either forgotten or unknown. When Roosevelt died in April 1945, my housekeeper—who was not given to emotion—brought me the news, crying help-lessly. There were people in tears all over London, that morning, going to work in their buses and underground trains. I have never seen such a flow of feeling in the town. It didn't happen when Churchill died. True, he was a very old man, his death was in the way of nature. Yet affection for him had grown as he passed into his old age. In his years of power it had not been spontaneous, nothing like the affection for Roosevelt: if Churchill had died when Roosevelt did, I am convinced that the mourning wouldn't have been spontaneous either.

He lived until he was over ninety. If he had died at sixty-five, he would have been one of the picturesque failures in English politics—a failure like his own father, Lord Randolph Churchill, or Charles James Fox. In fact, as early as the twenties, his staunch foul-weather friend, Max Beaverbrook—one of the most gifted friends he ever had—was already writing about him as a brilliant failure. His life, right up to the time when most men have finished, had been adventurous and twopence-colored, but he had achieved little. Except among his friends—and I mean his few real friends—he had never been popular. In most of his political life he had been widely and deeply disliked.

This dislike spread right outside politics. The four fellow-countrymen of his about whom I am writing in this book were all approximately contemporaries: Churchill born 1874, Lloyd George 1866, Wells 1866, Rutherford 1871, Hardy 1877. Lloyd George, as I have mentioned, had affection for him, but not really much respect. Wells caricatured him, in more than one novel, as a bombastic rhetorician, someone fixed in early militaristic adolescence, whose mind worked only like a gramophone (it is true that Wells, himself an extraordinarily inventive man, did at times respond to the inventive flair in Churchill). Rutherford, who saw a good deal of conservative politicians, shared their attitude towards him: and he went a bit further. Rutherford had the lowest possible opinion of Lindemann (a scientist *manqué*, said Rutherford): Lindemann was Churchill's intimate intellectual adviser: that put paid to the pair of them, so far as Rutherford's interest carried. As for Hardy, he, like many of the best minds in Edwardian Cambridge, had a generalized contempt for politicians as such (one could see traces of the same contempt in Russell, G. E. Moore, Keynes, and the whole Bloomsbury affiliation). Hardy was prepared to admit that Lloyd George was a test match player—a high term of praise. About Churchill, however, Hardy had not one good word to say. For Hardy, Churchill represented all the crassness and mindlessness of politics: he was the one person, in my long friendship with Hardy, who never drew from him some touch of fairness, humor or charity. I should record that Hardy thought highly of Lindemann's general intelligence.

They were all wrong, it doesn't need saying. But they came from different slices of intellectual England: and it did Churchill no good that he raised such emotions there. It did him and the rest of us no good, in a practical sense, when he came to power. For example, if his connections with Rutherford and the top scientists had not been so tenuous and peculiar—if they had been as good, say, as Macmillan's or Harold Wilson's—it is unthinkable that his meeting with Niels Bohr in 1944 should have been both a farce and a disaster. Bohr had begged for the meeting in order to explain the world-dangers of the atomic bomb, once it was made. Now Bohr was a physicist of great genius: he was also a profound and humane social thinker: he was one of the wisest men alive. But he was a prolix explicator of any subject: he was so anxious to leave out nothing of the truth that one had to be patient. He could, in short, be boring: but Rutherford, dead by 1944, or any of the great English scientists who had worked with Bohr could have explained to Churchill that one had to endure being bored: this was one of the most wonderful, and certainly one of the most humane, intelligences ever known. In fact, Churchill, having no such friends, was bored and worse than bored. He suspected that Bohr was some kind of subversive, and after the meeting wrote a minute suggesting that he ought to be put under house arrest. (Poor Bohr went away, shaking his great Danish head, thinking he was not good at communicating with politicians.)

The dislike of Churchill was just as strong among some of the high officials. Hankey had no use for him: this feeling was strongly reciprocated, with the result that I, who was working under Hankey, spent half the war watching him being pushed step by step down the ladder. They had not been on good terms in the 1914–18 war, and in the thirties had had a bitter private quarrel. One day in 1943 Hankey told me about it. He had taken me out to lunch in order to advise me not to take a job I had just been offered: he was, as usual, shrewd, and the advice was accepted. He was feeling more than customarily expansive. It was just after the battle of the Kursk salient, which, to anyone of military judgment, meant that the war must inevitably be won, and probably before too long. Hankey had by this time been pushed right off the ladder, but he was as single-minded a patriot as Churchill himself, and was happy because we were winning. So his discretion crumbled a little, and his humor, which was subfusc and self-deprecatory, broke through.

Winston Churchill ✳ 157

Yes, there had been a row. By the mid-thirties, he had been Secretary of the Cabinet for nearly twenty years. The Secretary of the Cabinet couldn't say much: he was anonymous: he couldn't assert himself. Suddenly—Hankey told me with a grin—he had felt obliged to assert himself for once. His was the one trained military mind near the Cabinet. Churchill was as usual bombinating on military matters. Churchill. Always an irritation: more an irritation than usual at that time: safely out of power: certain never to return. Hankey solemnly set to work to write a letter accusing Churchill of "debauching the young officers with talk and brandy" and of various other offenses against decorum and national well-being. Churchill was, not unnaturally, irate. "He did return to power," said Hankey mildly. Churchill, who was as a rule magnanimous and forgiving, did not forgive this time. Hankey had been in Chamberlain's War Cabinet: he then descended to Chancellor of the Duchy of Lancaster: then to Paymaster-General: then out.

I have heard some stories out of character in my life, but none more out of character than this. It would have been untypical for Hankey to say unnecessary rude words in a conversation: to do it *on paper* (a civil servant's major sin) seemed beyond belief. Yet he was the last man to invent a story.

Anyway, whether that letter exists or not, Churchill and Hankey did not view each other with approval. I mentioned, when writing about Lloyd George, that Hankey took a distinctly Tolstoyan view of history. Once —I think in that same summer of 1943—he startled a group of us by remarking that whoever had been in power, Chamberlain, Churchill, Halifax, Eden, anyone you liked to mention, the military position would now be *exactly the same*. Wars had their own rules, politicians didn't alter them, the armies would be in the same positions to the mile. I am moderately Tolstoyan myself, but I thought that was taking a mixture of anti-Churchillian and Tolstoyan thought remarkably far.

The result of that particular feud was that I spent a large part of the war in something like an opposition atmosphere. It was not until years later that I met people whose insight I respected, who were close to Churchill, and who regarded him, not only with admiration but with love. Edward Bridges was one of these (Hankey's successor as Secretary of the Cabinet): another was Harold Macmillan. When I listened to them talking about him, it was hard to remember that this was the man who had been so violently disliked. Yet he had been. It is difficult to detect exactly why. His egocentricity counted for a lot. But his whole temperament, and the life which his temperament forced him to live, did not fit his time: and he seems to have been hated for his virtues as much as for his faults. It is instructive to recall some of his career and see how often his major qualities, courage, magnanimity, imagination, brought him down, quite as heavily as his weaknesses.

He was born an aristocrat. In his childhood he was actually heir to his uncle, the Duke of Marlborough, until that none-too-agreeable figure managed to produce a son. If Churchill had in fact become a Duke, he, by the same complications which finally got him the Prime Ministership, would have been inevitably kept out: which is a curious irony, and which would have made a frustration of his life.

He had an unsatisfactory and unhappy boyhood. He was a textbook example of a highly intelligent person who just couldn't cope with a formal education. He had a high I.Q., as Volume I of his son's admirable biography clinchingly demonstrates, immense verbal though not mathematical aptitude, and gigantic, if latent, powers of concentration. The net result of these gifts was that he never got beyond a low form at Harrow. His father, Lord Randolph Churchill, who possessed a good deal of the ebullience, melancholy and egocentricity that his son was later to show, took no interest in him. Churchill worshipped his father, but got no affection back. With an indifferent impatience, Lord Randolph decided he had better become a soldier, since no one could think of anything else to do with him. Even then, though the standard of the entrance examination to Sandhurst must have been minimal, it gave him much difficulty to get through.

With the only piece of puritanical fervor that I can remember in the millions of words he produced, he remarks somewhere that Sandhurst was better for him than if he had gone to Oxford or Cambridge, because there he might have associated with "drunken scholars." This still seems a mysterious observation: no one ever accused him, at any time in his life, of being a really bigoted teetotaller. In fact, his drinking habits were one of the many odd things about him. He was in no sense an alcoholic: an alcoholic couldn't have drunk in the manner he did. He wasn't, in the technical sense, an obsessive drinker. He just drank day after day, every day and all day, all through his life.

He was not cut out to be a peace-time officer. He wanted glory, he wanted the excitement of war. He was a romantic born (I believe this was an aspect of his temperament that put some people off). His physical courage (or any other kind of courage) no one, except possibly himself, ever doubted. I inserted that qualification, "except possibly himself," in an article that was printed some years ago. I did it after re-reading his memoirs with closer textual attention. It seemed clear that he had the highest kind of courage, the kind that exists superposed on an active and anxious imagination. When I read Lord Moran's book, I found him noting that Churchill, though so brave, was also apprehensive—deliberately taking risky war-time airtrips, and then worrying about the chances of fire: anxious about all kinds of danger, and then running into them. There are, of course, people who don't know fear. They are enviable, but they don't attract our moral admiration: they are just lucky. The admirable type of courage is that which Churchill had, and which he shared with his commanders, Alexander and Montgomery. It is a pity, I have often thought, that people did not come to realize that Churchill was often apprehensive: they would have liked him more.

Now that I have mentioned Lord Moran's book, I want to add something else. The ethics of its being published are not my concern. But I should like to say that of all the streams of words that have been written or spoken about Churchill, Lord Moran's and his son's are the only ones which have taught me anything about the man himself. His character was abnormally impenetrable to most kinds of insight: there were sharp observers round him, but of his later life only Lord Moran has managed to tell us much.

As a young man he longed—one is now sure that he had anxieties which no one else guessed—to know what danger felt like. In the Victorian afternoon of the British Empire, he managed to work in a lot of military activity in improbable places, in India, in Egypt (where he took part in one of the last cavalry charges), in South Africa (where he was taken prisoner by the Boers, escaped and was accused—unjustly but with the ill-luck that pursued him until he was an old man—of breaking his parole).

Then politics. He entered Parliament at the age of twenty-seven, and within a remarkably short space of time became the most hated politician in the country, with the honorable exception of Lloyd George. He started as a conservative, which in essence he always was. Soon he changed his party. In English politics this has always taken some living down. In Churchill's case it took even more living down, because his change was shortly afterwards followed by the great liberal victory of 1906, and Churchill found himself a member of the liberal administration, the most gifted this country has ever had.

From that day his name was a dirty word in respectable conservative circles, and stayed so for a long time. One could still meet elderly conservatives, after his wartime dominance, who in their hearts could not bring themselves to approve of him. They had always thought that he was arrogant, ambitious, an adventurer. He was an aristocrat, but he preferred the company of other adventurers. They even thought him tricky and dishonest (like a copy of their *bête noire*, Lloyd George)—whereas in fact his character was upright and bone-rigid, and he was a most undexterous politician.

For years he could do nothing quite right. He was an excellent First Lord of the Admiralty before and at the beginning of the First World War. But his best ideas came to nothing. He was responsible for the development of the tank (which H. G. Wells had brilliantly anticipated on paper in 1903), but the weapon was wasted. His major strategic conception, Gallipoli, was probably a fine idea: but once again it brought defeat. This was partly because he had made a bad personal choice in recalling Fisher as First Sea Lord: and partly also, one sometimes suspects, because the plan contained too many logistic variables to start an even chance with the resources of that war.

In the war-time coalitions, the conservatives made it their first condition that Churchill should not hold high office. When Lloyd George became Prime Minister, he, the most persuasive of men, had to struggle for months to smuggle Churchill in: even then, Lloyd George, who was paying a debt of gratitude, had to take one of his bigger risks.

So Churchill went through his middle-age. The record of brilliant failures got longer. He changed his party again and rejoined the Tories. Not that that helped much. He enjoyed himself, much too flamboyantly, in suppressing the General Strike of 1926. He had a lively but unsuccessful spell as Chancellor of the Exchequer (1924–29). After that, the one point on which all conservatives were agreed was that he had to be kept out of office at all costs. The only dissentients were a few up-and-coming men far to the conservative left, such as Eden, Macmillan, Bracken, Boothby: but most of these were distrusted and kept out of office themselves. In the thirties Churchill seemed to most of official England the classical case of a man with a brilliant future behind him. He was the chief conservative critic of the conservative government—passionately opposed to them over India (where he behaved like a romantic nineteenth century imperialist and was dead wrong), over their lack of preparation for war and their attempts to appease Hitler (where he was dead right).

Thus he managed, until he was old, to be disapproved of, for quite different reasons, by the right and by the left. To the left, in particular to the English working class, he was simply a reactionary. I doubt whether they minded his stand over India: the English working class are very insular: but they have memories like elephants, and they did not forget his antics in the General Strike. Still, he was on their side against Hitler. It was they—or at least some of them, including the toughest trade union leaders —who wanted him in power in the thirties, to show that the country was not going to give in. It was their spokesmen who, by refusing on any conditions to serve under Chamberlain, finally forced Churchill into power. In his war-time reign, they were completely loyal. I don't think the mass of labor voters exactly loved him, either then or at any time, except maybe in 1940. But they had come to respect him, and they followed him.

Nevertheless, anyone used to drinking in London

pubs and talking to service men before the 1945 election could not be surprised when he was thrown out of office. The soldiers had their heroes, such as Montgomery, but Churchill was not one of them. He was neither an electoral asset nor a liability, and his name, over the whole political scene, probably didn't affect twenty seats. This has, of course, been true of most Prime Ministers. As a rule, the electorate in this country vote for parties, not for people. The mass of the population wanted sweeping social reforms, and, with a surge of feeling, decided that the conservative party could not make them. So nothing and no one—not a combination of the supreme politicians of democratic history, Lincoln, Franklin Roosevelt, Lloyd George—could have saved it.

On the right, among his own kind and his own party, the distrust of Churchill in the thirties was more serious. Over Hitler and the war to come he was telling them the harshest of truths: but even so, the passion of feeling against him came from deeper roots than disagreement. Some of those roots were discreditable: they came from sheer blind envy. At that time Churchill was the most miscellaneously gifted man in politics. He had the kind of aristocratic magnanimity which, instead of reducing the amount of envy, seemed to provoke it. (It is no use forgiving someone handsomely if you don't care a damn who he is or what he has done.) He behaved like a prince, at a time when princely behavior had gone right out of fashion. He was not good at dealing with the high officials. He had no social contacts with them, which most politicians find desirable—just as he had few contacts with the academics. This is a country where the high officials and the academics are interlinked, and more powerful than in any other. His habits were not theirs, they did not like his friends.

All that might have been trivial. He was too distinguished, he was envied, he didn't get on with lesser men. But they had one rational criticism of him. There was something in it. I now believe that it shows up something in his personality which did him great harm and yet which, at the moment of trial, turned into a virtue. It consists, on the superficial level, of one word—"judgment," or rather lack of it. For forty years of public life, the orthodox remark in England was: "Churchill? Brilliant, of course. But no judgment."

"Judgment," to people concerned with political decisions, means two things—one which most of us would think good, one bad. The bad thing is the ability to guess what everyone else is thinking, and think like them. This Churchill never had, and would have despised himself for having. But the good thing in "judgment" is the ability to think of many matters at once, in their interdependence, their relative importance, and their consequences. In this sense, I don't think there is any burking the fact that Churchill's judgment was, on a great many occasions in his life, seriously defective.

Even when he came to power. Compare him with an admirable but far less brilliant man, the United States Chief of Staff, George Marshall. With both of them sitting round a table, he seemed inarticulate, almost dull, by the side of Churchill. No one could claim for Marshall, least of all himself, any of the sparks of imaginative genius that Churchill emitted, whatever he was touching. Yet, in the affairs which they were jointly tackling, Marshall's judgment was, not always but usually, by long odds the better. The history of World War II has yet to be written. Churchill's memoirs are marvellously attractive and convincing. As one reads them, one is entirely on his side. But, now the military critics are getting to work, it seems likely that, over a good many crises of judgment, history won't be.

Churchill had a very powerful mind, but a romantic and unquantitative one. If he thought about a course of action long enough, if he conceived it alone in his own inner consciousness and desired it passionately, he convinced himself that it must be possible. Then, with incomparable invention, eloquence and high spirits, he set out to convince everyone else that it was not only possible, but the only course of action open to man. Unfortunately, the brute facts of life were not always too malleable to his listeners.

That obsessive quality of his temperament drove him into his major errors, both in war and peace. Think of his famous cry: "I have not become the King's First Minister in order to preside over the dissolution of the British Empire." Resounding, yes. The grand manner, yes. But as his American allies knew better than he did, it didn't make sense. Any Prime Minister, however imperialistic, however strong-willed, would have been obliged to preside over the dissolution of the Empire. If we had tried to hold India in any shape or form, after 1945, it would not only have been morally wrong, it would have been plain fatuous. India would have gone anyway, with suffering on both sides and with bitterness which we have, on the whole, been spared.

Yet ironically this same obsessive quality, which often distorted his judgment and led him into errors, was also the force which drove him into the cardinal achievement of his life. Judgment is a fine thing: but it is not all that uncommon. Deep insight is much rarer. Churchill had flashes of that kind of insight, dug up from his own nature, independent of influences, owing nothing to anyone outside himself. Sometimes it was a better guide than judgment: in the ultimate crisis when he came to power, there were times when judgment itself could, though it did not need to, become a source of weakness.

When Hitler came to power, Churchill did not use judgment, but one of his deep insights. This was absolute danger, there was no easy way round. *That* was what we needed. It was a unique occasion in our history. It had to be grasped by a nationalist leader. Plenty of people on the left could see the danger: but they did not know how the country had to be seized and unified.

Not many men in conservative England had such insight. Churchill had.* As poor Ralph Wigram, one of the ablest young diplomats, said shortly before he killed himself, in despair because he could not convince the politicians what Hitler meant, "Anyway, there's Winston. We must leave it to Winston. He is strong, he knows it all, he will go on to the end."

I have just suggested that he had a kind of insight,

* So had Lindemann, who saw the Hitler danger as clearly as Churchill himself. I wish I had made this major service clear, when I was criticizing Lindemann on other grounds.

dug up from his own nature, independent of influences, owing nothing to anyone outside himself. Such insight, which is itself extremely rare, usually occurs inextricably mixed up with abnormal egocentricity. It was so with Churchill, who was not a saint. It may have been so, in a beautiful and sublimated form, with Einstein, who was nearer a saint than most men: but he too owed nothing to a living soul and was as unbudgeable as Churchill. But with Churchill the egocentricity was aggressive; it gave him his force, it was linked with his insight, and perhaps was linked with the personal aura, the climate of dislike, that surrounded him until he was old. As Moran remarks, he hadn't antennae to probe other people. What was more, he didn't see any special reason why he should have. Massive, witty, inconsiderate, he was sufficient for himself.

Some people, not necessarily hero-worshippers, can be attracted to such a character. But others, particularly those who are prone to self-regard and who are sensitive to pique, feel the opposite of attracted: and the majority of the human race are regrettably prone to self-regard and sensitive to pique. This was unfortunate for Churchill, and—when one thinks of what he might have saved us in the thirties—unfortunate for us all.

And yet, in his old age, he sweetened English life. His second Prime Ministership, from 1951–55, was harder for him than the first: he was getting on for eighty, he could not bear new faces, and so insisted on keeping the officials he had known. When at last he retired, he seems to have passed into long patches of an old man's melancholy: certainly, at odd meetings about the founding of Churchill College, I never saw him smile—which would have been unthinkable only a few years before. But the legends which were collecting round him had nothing of the sadness of his actual old age. By another paradox, this time one which made amends for past injustice, the ripples which percolated to the public of the surviving Churchill, were ripples of the picturesque and noble qualities which, when he was in full vigor, many people had not wanted to see.

Somehow, those picturesque and noble qualities began to seem something the country was starved of. His memoirs might be one-sided as a historical source, but they were, beyond all quibbling, the work of a singularly magnanimous man. And we had run short of magnanimity: it was good to recognize it in him. Too much of our life had become sour and malicious. That he had never been. For the last ten years of his life, his broad and expansive virtues were remembered. He had become a myth, and a handsome myth, in his own lifetime. Whether it comforted him at all, no one can be sure: but it certainly comforted some of the rest of us.

At long last, he got the recognition for his great deeds. With a few exceptions he had forgiven his enemies. He had been the loyalest of friends, and had taken great risks for those he loved. He stood by Lloyd George and Edward VIII in the hardest crises of their lives: he had paid a heavy price for his chivalry, but years later people enjoyed the thought of it. They *enjoyed*, in fact, the thought of how he had lived his life. The Corinthian gusto, the brandy and champagne, the determination to do exactly what he wanted, come hell, come high water:

on the other hand, the happy and decorous marriage. No one could recall hearing a breath of sexual scandal about him. Which, considering how many enemies had been out to finish him, seemed astonishing in itself.

I did once hear an anecdote for which I have no evidence. I heard it during the war: like those cumulating stories in his last ten years, it left a pleasant taste.

It was told me by a charming elderly woman, now dead, who had herself been a dashing beauty in Edwardian society. She had just come back from a railway journey. The time was the middle of the war, when Churchill was at the peak of his power. She found herself in a carriage with another elderly woman, an acquaintance whom she had not met for a long time. According to my informant this was the woman Churchill in his twenties had wanted to marry (long before he met his future wife). She had been smart, pretty, an heiress: the only difficulty was that she had not returned his love. He had pursued her with the single-mindedness that he later spent on war: he proposed to her in country house after country house as the old Queen's reign was coming to an end. He had used all his eloquence, all his force, every resource he had. None of it was any good. She finally married someone who happened to have a very common English name—I will call him Mr. Smith—and who was otherwise unknown to history. So my informant sat opposite Mrs. Smith, whom she had not met since they were both young women, in the railway carriage. There was a good deal of chat about old times. Then my informant said:

"You must be very proud of your old flame."

"What do you mean?"

"Mr. Churchill, of course."

At that Mrs. Smith is said to have given a gentle non-committal smile. My informant could not resist asking:

"Come now, have you never wished that you had married him?"

Then Mrs. Smith looked her straight in the eye, and said:

"My dear Nellie, if Mr. Churchill had ever done me the honor of asking me to marry him, I should of course have accepted him on the spot."

That might have come straight out of Anthony Hope, I thought. Too gallant to believe? Anyway, such was the story. I cannot vouch for any part of it. But from the point of view of the Churchillian apotheosis, it doesn't matter whether it is true or not. It does carry the tone of high-hearted behavior, higher-hearted behavior than we could manage in our own time. And it was Churchill's own high-hearted behavior that became the substance of his myth. People wanted something to admire that seemed to be smothered among the grit of everyday. Whatever could be said against him, he had virtues, graces, style. Courage, magnanimity, loyalty, wit, gallantry—these were not often held up for admiration in our literature, or indeed depicted at all. He really had them. I believe that it was deep intuition which made people feel, in those last ten years, that his existence had after all sweetened English life.

ROBERT FROST

A FEW months after Robert Frost's death, I had an engagement at the Foreign Languages Library in Moscow. I saw a notice inside, advertising a memorial lecture about him that night: and so, either before or after my own date, I forget which, I went in to listen. I know that, right at the end of his life, he had paid a visit to Russia which was more of a triumph than that of any American writer in living memory. Yevtushenko, who had taken him round, had loved him. So had the other poets. So had the audiences he had talked to. He had at last been splendidly translated into Russian, I was told. Writing like his, simple on the surface, is nearly always a translator's nightmare (this is true, in reverse, of Tvardovsky, who is something of a Russian equivalent to Frost) : it is the ornamented and baroque which is easiest to translate. However, the problem had been solved. His poetry was now known all over the country. Writer and man, they had taken him to themselves.

173

I had met him myself several times, first in England during a similar triumphal tour of his, six years before. Old, strong, pawky, witty, he had made more immediate impact on undergraduate listeners than any writer I could remember. I had heard a bit about him in America, and had become extremely interested. I wanted to hear what the Russians made of him.

The memorial lecture, which was one of several in his honor, was curiously moving. It was given by a Lithuanian poet. The room was packed: there must have been several hundred people present. They were reverential, utterly attentive. On the green baize at the top table stood a large photograph of the familiar face. Close by, titles visible to the room, were sets of Frost, in English and Russian. The lecturer was eloquent, passionate, full of knowledge and understanding of the poetry. It was poetry, he said, that sprang from profound experience, from the deepest feeling for life. It was not symbolic in a crude sense: and yet the poet used concrete images, which had a real existence in everyday terms, to carry a universal meaning. This was what the greatest masters of Russian verse, English verse, had always done—Pushkin himself. The audience were raptly following the quotations, some of them in English. And then the lecturer went on to say that "our friend whom we are lamenting" was not only a poet of high talent (this sounds luke-warm, but Russians don't normally distinguish between genius and talent—it is common to hear someone speak of, for example, Tolstoy's talent), but a man of the most warm and generous heart. He was a friend of our country. He was a friend of peace. He had both humor and wisdom. He had lived to a great age, tranquil, kind, loving his fellow-men, giving them joy. Above all, he was a good man.

The audience applauded with emotion. There were tears in many eyes. It was the kind of response that a memorial lecture to Frost would have elicited either in England or America, but, this being a Russian audience, more unrestrained. An English memorial lecture would, in fact, have followed similar lines. I found myself at a disadvantage when, later that night, this one was being discussed among some Russian friends. Frost's poetry—yes. I genuinely admired that, though with some qualifications that they wouldn't make. As for the rest, I didn't really know much about him until I read the Untermeyer correspondence a year later. But I did know one or two things. It was no use talking to them about what his politics really were. In fact, just by the influence of his personality he had done good to American-Soviet relations, and that was splendid. Leave well alone. They loved him: at the age of eighty-six he had come to believe in co-existence (but not until then, I thought in secret): that was good enough. As for his character, they had inspected him from all angles, as Russians, the most indefatigable of psychological observers, tend to do. Some of my friends were as subtle as Frost was himself. Often they saw deeper than the rest of us. This time, for once, they seemed to me to be over-simplifying.

And yet, I thought later, though they were wrong in detail they were right to respond to him as one of the deepest-natured of men. He had lived a life of passionate experience, right up to the end. He had been through great suffering. Emotionally he had known everything.

He was not a specially good man: by the standards of Einstein or Hardy, he was not a good man at all. He was neither magnanimous nor serene. To himself he never controlled his temperament. He was both complex and extravagantly devious. He never did anything he didn't want to do: under a mask of helplessness, he spared nobody in getting—not everything, but almost everything he wanted. He was capable of acting, stripping off façade after façade like onion-skins. He was sometimes a bit of a fraud. His character was altogether more variegated, more heterogeneous in its structure, than that of any of the others in this book. At the root of his nature, he was as independent as it is given a man to be.

Much of what I have just said we now know for certain. It is different from, and often contradictory of, the public persona he maintained for so long. When I first met him, I, like most other people, thought that this public persona was closely similar to his inner self. His personality had great attractiveness. It was pleasant to take it at its persona value—and to think of a writer simple, intensely shrewd, but above the battle. When one knew him a little better, the attractiveness remained but that illusion didn't: one at least realized that he was a subtle man, with a nature difficult either to reach or comprehend. If it hadn't been for a singular accident, it is doubtful whether any but his intimates would have got any nearer comprehension now. Simple. Above the battle. We have his own word for it that he was about as simple as Marcel Proust, and as much above the battle as Lloyd George in his more active moods.

The singular accident was that he happened to be an

obsessive letter writer, and had one intimate and admiring friend. For nearly fifty years he wrote letters to Louis Untermeyer: and it is one of the most interesting correspondences (a one-sided correspondence, for either Frost didn't keep, or Untermeyer has chosen not to publish, Untermeyer's own side) in literary history. Untermeyer was ten years the younger man. He was a good poet and critic, with tastes that—in a formal sense—were antimodernist. He was one of the first Americans to become a Frost partisan—this was when Frost was unknown in his own country. Untermeyer remained Frost's most devoted and tireless champion until death, and became also a beautifully selfless friend. In some circles Frost was once regarded as one of the saints of literature: that view is no longer tenable, and if either of them is to have the title, Untermeyer deserves it more. As a rule, incidentally, it is the junior partner in the major literary alliances who turns out to be the finer character: Eckermann was a better man than Goethe, and Max Brod than Kafka.

Untermeyer had an awful lot to put up with. He was himself a man of generous impulses: he was a sincere and dedicated liberal: he had to endure year after year Frost's dark, often extreme, and sometimes cruelly unfeeling conservatism. Much worse, Untermeyer's own troubles—and there were a good many—were submerged by Frost's. That was natural when Frost's harsh tragedies were on him. But even Frost's minor difficulties had a knack of becoming more totally pressing than Untermeyer's major ones. Quite often in the letters Frost apologizes for his egotism. He experienced genuine remorse, as he experienced everything else: but it didn't seem to have much effect on his future behavior. Yet, at the end of it all, Untermeyer had two rewards, and no one ever deserved them more. He enjoyed a trust and friendship that Frost gave to no one else (except perhaps to Edward Thomas, for a very short period in England): and Frost, though not a particularly likable man as one got closer to him, was almost certainly in intimacy a lovable one. The second reward was artistic, and Untermeyer was one of the born servants of the arts. As a result of long-suffering, of sheer goodness, he received a literary record that is one of the great documents of self-revelation. Here all Frost's onion-skin façades are, deliberately, stripped away. Nearly all—not quite all, but nearly—dissimulations are kicked aside. In one of his contradictory aspects, Frost, who was capable of lying, was also capable of savage honesty. These letters contain passages of introspective insight that make most introspective writers look as though they were making self-indulgent excuses for themselves.

Perhaps a warning may be needed. For these passages of insight alone, the letters have great value, not only for people interested in Frost himself, but in human experience: and there are many other passages, from a mind of exceptional nonconformity, which teach one a lot about literature and the literary life, which give one the impression that no one has ever thought about these problems before. But to find those passages the reader has to do some work: for they are embedded in a plasma of facetiousness, partly cracker barrel, partly academic. His enemy Ezra Pound had a not dissimilar kind of facetiousness. Untermeyer obviously enjoyed Frost's brand, and calls it his "extraordinary playfulness." I shouldn't have enjoyed it at all: even now, it makes my jaw ache.

I said that Frost was capable of lying. He was certainly capable of fantastication, even in old age: there is the well-known story of his confrontation with T. S. Eliot in Boston when Frost claimed, quite untruthfully, to have composed a poem on the spot. It even seems likely that, for most of his life, he fantasticated about the date of his birth.

Actually, he was born in San Francisco in 1874. For a great many years he put the date one year later: then, in his late seventies, announced that he had discovered a mistake. He must be the only famous man who has had his 80th birthday celebrations four years after his 75th. Some of this story strains the credulity a bit. Why didn't he know when he was born? If he had emerged, like Stalin, from the darkest poverty of Tsarist Georgia, it might make sense: though in fact Stalin's birthday is accurately marked in the church records. Frost's origins were, however, neither illiterate nor poverty-stricken. His father had got his Phi Beta Kappa at Harvard: he was working, during his son's childhood, as a journalist on the *San Francisco Bulletin*. His own parents were middle-class New Englanders. His wife was a Scottish girl who had been teaching in high schools in Ohio. She was educated, conscientious and deeply religious. One would require some convincing that such a family had forgotten the year of birth of their only son. The story reminds me of an old friend of mine, a professional cricketer, who in his thirties suddenly thought that his chances of selection for

Robert Frost ❧ 179

test matches would be improved if he were two years younger: so in the Births columns of Wisden (the official record of the game), his date of birth mysteriously changed from 1888 to 1890. No one appeared to ask any questions. He duly got chosen for test matches.

Some Americans, who have a beady eye for dissimulation, have made fun of Frost's creation of his own origins. From the beginning of his poetic life he became, as it were, a professional New Englander, a child of the rocky soil, a farmer of farmers, or (the description he liked to use in old age) a Vert from Vermont. Sceptical voices point out that he was born in California: and that, if his father hadn't died young, when the boy was eleven, he would have stayed there at least till he was grown up. Then what about the New England myth? This seems to be less than fair. His father's family were genuine, aboriginal New Englanders, generations of them with English names. Presumably they had once been farmers, like all the seventeenth century settlers. They had long since ceased to be so; farming was his own romantic invention, which we shall come to later. In fact, his ancestors had come into the towns as soon as New England became industrialized. His grandfather Frost had been modestly successful as overseer in a mill at Lawrence, Massachusetts, a town about as rural as nineteenth century Halifax or Huddersfield: he had made, or saved, some money, and was tight with it in a good New England or Yorkshire fashion. But money was always there, for purposes the grandfather considered good, such as sending Robert on what turned out to be unsuccessful academic expeditions to Dartmouth and Harvard. It was to Lawrence that Frost's mother, with the two children, moved when his father died. She made a living by running a private school at Salem close by, and then in Lawrence itself. In between high school terms, Frost, like many American boys, did a variety of jobs in the local factories. His whole adolescence was passed in the black industrial townscape—though, so far as I recollect, there is only one poem which admits its existence. To find an English writer's equivalent of Frost's youth, the nearest might be Priestley's in Bradford twenty years later.

Frost was a success in high school, apart from a re-markable (and life-long) inability to spell. Intellectually he was head of his class: he was proficient at games, to which he remained devoted into old age: he had already a striking physical presence. Even when he was a very old man, one noticed his eyes: the irises were white-rimmed, as they become in extreme age, but the color had not all faded. In his youth, they were a dazzling blue. He may have known, unusually early, that he had charm for women. He fell in love in his teens with a class-mate, a clever and beautiful girl, and married her at twenty-one. It was a deep and passionate marriage, indissoluble until her death over forty years later. During it, they under-went much suffering, she so much that one wants to turn one's head away.

As soon as he left high school, Frost had given clear signs that he wouldn't do anything he didn't want to do. He was thought to be lazy: did he understand that being lazy was a particularly good cover? That, in secret, he had already made up his mind, and nothing was going to shift him? At that age—though later he understood his own instinctive cunning well enough—it probably wasn't clear, even to him. He may have realized that he didn't relish competition: he had the sort of pride that makes it intolerable not to win. And so, when he was sent to Dartmouth, then as now a first-class liberal arts college, where there must have been clever young men who could have given him something to measure himself against, he returned after three months—in order to perform the unexacting task of helping his mother with her private school. He wouldn't find a job, he wouldn't compete: though, by a sardonic irony, as soon as he started his poetic career he became, in the depth of his nature, as competitive as any poet could be and stayed so, at much cost to himself, until he died.

He was quite young when he knew that he wanted to be a poet. He wrote poems and had some published in obscure magazines (not little magazines in the modern sense). He got almost no money for them, nor from any other poems he wrote until he was over forty. He didn't know whether he was any good. In a profound sense, it is possible that he never knew whether he was any good. His letters contain many flashes of self-doubt. How much of his poetry had any value? Did any of it? These dark patches are, of course, common in most writers: but in him they were unusually pervading, and the doubt gnawed very deep. Often he was begging for reassurance. It was this need for reassurance which made him so compulsively competitive and which gave the bite to his rivalry with T. S. Eliot: a one-sided rivalry, incidentally, for there is no sign that Eliot acknowledged its existence, or had any special interest in Frost at all. It was certainly this need for reassurance that for Frost made the award of the Nobel Prize a yearly agony—until, in his last year of life, at the age of 88, he thought it was coming and was, for the last time, deprived.

Whatever his doubts about his own value, he had none at all about the romantic conception of the artist, or the manner in which an artist—that is, himself—should live his life. This was on the surface one of his contradictions, for he spent so much time appearing to deny it. The plain farmer from New England, faithfully married, good citizen—what had he in common with the romantic artists who didn't admit any obligations, whom he disliked and despised? The short answer is, almost everything. Even being a farmer was romantic, in a sense which didn't help his poetry. Much more, he believed, as much as Verlaine, that art was its own justification. That a life spent in writing poetry needed no other excuse. That his first duty was to write poetry. That, for the sake of writing poetry, everything else must of necessity be sacrificed. His own well-being must be sacrificed: that was fairly easy, as it would be for most writers if pushed, simply because writing poetry brought its own well-being. The well-being of everyone round him, wife, children, friends, must be sacrificed: that was not so easy, but it did not deter him.

When he married, he was still teaching at his mother's private school. Soon afterwards he had another shot at a university education, and persuaded his grandfather to support him at Harvard. But this didn't for long fit his conception of the writing life, and he left in his second year. Once again grandfather was called on. Would he buy him a farm? So at twenty-six he was installed in a small New Hampshire farm, the first of his New England farms, the beginning of the farmer-poet persona.

It was a romantic and literary persona. Partly it was composed out of the conventional anti-industrialism of his literary contemporaries, perhaps even stronger in the United States than England (and strong, of course, still: I remember a very intelligent young woman, of literary talent, leaning out of a tenth storey window somewhere near Riverside Drive and saying with intense feeling, "Plough up the wretched sidewalks! Plough them all up!" I was impressed by her emotion, but it did not strike me as the most helpful way to deal with urban civilization). It was a stereotype to feel like doing a Thoreau. Frost did it. Just because it was a stereotype, it was, as Yvor Winters has pointed out, injurious to his poetry. He set himself to get rid of romantic influences. When he was writing from the depth of his nature, he succeeded. But sometimes, more marked because of the starkness he was striving for, there is the pseudo-archaic, the pseudo-Georgic, sticking out like a sore thumb. In this, he often resembles A. E. Housman. Frost's best poems did what he wanted: but, reading the introspective flashes of his letters, one can't help longing for the poems he might have written. No one showed more or shrewder suspicion of the literary climate of his time: but he could not utterly free himself from it, as Yeats did in old age. He did not trust enough in his own ultimate originality, which was potentially as unique as Yeats's.

"Doing well is all that matters," he said with his hard-grained sense. If you're going to be a farmer, be a good farmer. Most of his aphorisms were as tough as that. He was not, however, a good farmer. He used to admit this with sardonic humor late in life. He made no money at it: he did not pay his way one single year. In fact, though he went on calling himself a farmer, he gave up the attempt, except as a hobby, after four years. From that time on he earned his family's living by various kinds of teaching: to begin with in local schools, and later in colleges. He was the first large-scale poet-in-residence. Until he was fifty, he couldn't have kept alive on his poetry: but he was saved, not by that romantic establishment the farm, but by the patronage—the abnormally good-tempered patronage, for he wasn't above taking advantage of his position—of American universities.

Even if he had been a dedicated farmer (he wasn't: he suffered from the professional disadvantage of not being prepared, or able, to get up in the morning), he couldn't have made a go of it. Farming in Vermont and New Hampshire in the 1900's wasn't a game for amateurs. It might just be feasible for French-Canadians with large families, bred to the harsh earth, all working every hour of the day. But sensible Anglo-Saxons, probably including some of Frost's own forebears, had fifty years before he was born decided that farming in New England was a foolish business, when there was good land out in Ohio or on the other side of the Mississippi. If he had really intended to be a serious farmer, that's where he would have gone. Those Virgilian Vermont farms were suitable places for prosperous New Yorkers to lose money—as the unfortunate Untermeyer discovered when, impressed by Frost's propaganda but not apparently by his experience, he became a farmer himself.

Nevertheless, though the Thoreau-inspired years were not professional, they meant hardship. No money was coming in. The family didn't have much to eat. It was poverty. Poverty *voulu*, if you like, since there was always money in the background, and if he ceased to live up to his romantic conception his grandfather would help him. But Frost took the hardship. So did his wife: it was much worse than hardship for her. She was utterly lonely. She had to provide for a family at the subsistence-level. He was self-absorbed. It is difficult to guess how good a father he was at that stage: as a very old man he was adept with children. But he certainly felt remorse for the life he had inflicted on his wife, and for the fates which, with Sophoclean inexorability, ruined his family.

Whether he could have warded off some of those fates, no one can know. There was something defective in the genes of the Frost family. His father died of tuberculosis at 34. His only sister became insane. He himself, though he survived to a robust old age, was thought in his youth to have his father's disease, and for long periods, even when he had won the fame he wanted and the storms were over, lived somewhere near the edge of neurotic invalidism. He had six children, two boys and four girls. The elder boy died in infancy, and so did the youngest daughter. The effect on his wife (and the gap in feeling between them) shows through in "Home Burial," one of his deepest poems. Of the other four, the favorite daughter had a history of illness, including tuberculosis, recovered, and then died in childbirth. Another daughter, after an unhappy marriage, relapsed into a state of neurotic withdrawal. The second son, after failing both at farming and poetry, became a paranoiac-depressive in his thirties and shot himself. The Eumenides had done their work thoroughly. Only one of the children, the eldest daughter, fought her way through into active life.

Frost's wife was herself dead before her son's suicide, which was the last of the fatalities. She had been more afflicted than she could accept: the death of the beloved daughter was an intolerable loss: she could not be reconciled to what had happened, nor wish to be. Frost wrote of her: "I have had almost too much of her suffering in this world." For himself, he behaved with stoical resignation, except when his wife died. Years before he had offhandedly made what was perhaps an ominous prophecy about himself . . . . "they [poets] are much less sensitive from having over-used their sensibilities. Men who have to feel for a living would unavoidably become altogether unfeeling except professionally." Some of his children's tragedies he seems to have borne with more composure than many men would. Yet, when his wife died—they were both in their mid-sixties—he became something like unhinged. Talking, drinking (for the only time in his life), resigning jobs, deranged, he spent months on the blasted heath. Before a year had gone by, he was writing "Be moderately sorry for a poor old man of iron will. Nothing I do or say is as yet due to anything but a strong determination to have my own way. I may show as sick, but it is for practical purposes. I don't know what I deserve for a nature like mine. I was boasting . . . this very day that I was clever enough to beat my nature."

Those culminating disasters happened when he had

achieved fame, at least in the English-speaking world, reputation, though not quite the reputation he struggled for, security, some money. A great deal had accrued to him—but it had been a long time coming. He was forty before anything came at all. He had gone on publishing poems in magazines now forgotten: he had gone on teaching in New Hampshire schools: no one cared much what he did. No critic had said a word about his poetry.

Then it occurred to him to go to England. His grandfather had died, leaving a trust which would be dealt out to him in small instalments. His poverty, it is worth repeating, had never become the real precipice-edge thing, when you have no one in the world to look to but yourself: Wells or Rutherford could have told him what that meant. Frost could pay for wife and family, move to England, take a country cottage. Within a few months he had found a publisher for his first volume of poems, been taken up by Ezra Pound, and had a critical success.

It sounds easy. It is pleasant for an Englishman to know that it happened in England. But it is not difficult to explain, and English literary circles ought not to be given any inordinate credit. By this time he had written some very good poems: once they were collected, this was a talent that didn't take much of an eye to spot. Further, he was in some superficial senses writing in the tone of the Georgian poets: he was much better than they were and his final work was different in kind from theirs (the only permissible English comparison would be Thomas Hardy), but they took him for one of themselves. As for Ezra Pound, he was at that time one of the most generous of talent-spotters. He and Frost soon quarrelled. Pound wanted Frost to write poetry according to the Pound rules, and Frost was the last man in the world to write— or do anything else—according to any rules but his own. For the rest of their careers they became literary enemies. But Pound helped give him a start, on both sides of the Atlantic. Many years later, after two wars, Frost repaid that debt, when he, as much as any man, was responsible for getting Pound discharged from the Bethesda asylum. It is said that Frost returned to friends, having made his appeal for Pound, conscious of having done his duty, proud of being the spokesman of poetry, and observed: "And I didn't even like the man."

With his second volume, *North of Boston,* Frost had another and a bigger success. In England his name was made for good (it took another year for the book—his first collection in America—to be published in New York). He was forty years of age. The date was April 1914.

He returned home the following year. His time in England had established him as a poet. It had also given him, with Edward Thomas, a friendship of beautiful quality: if it had not been for Frost's influence, Thomas's poetry would not have been written. Yet Frost didn't like either England or the English much. His attitude altered somewhat in his extreme old age: he was nothing if not human, and his triumphant reception in England in 1957 made him feel there might be something to be said for the country after all (he felt the same about Russia after his triumph there). But for almost the whole of his life he didn't really like us.

Whether this is surprising or not, I don't know.

Robert Frost ✻ 189

There has always been something asymmetrical about Anglo-American relationships. Speaking for myself—but it is also true of many Englishmen who have spent a good deal of time in America—I find it impossible to feel a foreigner there. I know all about the differences, I have lived in parts of the United States which would seem unfamiliar to most Americans. Nevertheless, I don't feel foreign. This means that one tends to take the same liberties as in one's own country: one is as free with one's criticism, much more so than in, say, Holland or Sweden, countries much more like England in their social structure.

Frost would have thought, in fact did think, as can be seen from a continual trickle of complaints in his letters, that taking such liberties was ill-mannered. Englishmen might not feel foreigners in America, but they were foreigners to him: and he, in reverse, felt a foreigner in England. It seems a little strange. After all, in name, in racial origin, in religion, his ancestors were indistinguishable from those of his English acquaintances. Yet this asymmetry was real for him, and for a lot of Americans of his generation. It may be weakening now. Sometimes I suspect it was specially strong in those of Anglo-Saxon stock. Some of the Americans who have understood England most naturally, accepted us as we accept ourselves, and taken the liberties which we take in America, have had origins quite different from Frost's.

England had established him at 40. He still had over half his life to live. Until an advanced age (very rare for a poet of his kind) he went on writing poetry. To himself, that was justification, it was the inner purity of his existence. In practical terms, he was fairly cunning in looking after himself. He still called himself a farmer: in succession, he owned five New England farms: but he did not spend much time on them. Like most good writers, particularly those with a romantic conception of their calling, he was an excellent business man, a very much better business man than farmer (and incidentally a very much better business man than Wells, and Arnold Bennett, who prided themselves on being so). He obtained an annual stipend from his publishers, until at the age of 50 or so, money began to flow in from his poetry, not in great sums, but probably more than to any modern English-language poet except Eliot.* Though he drove tough New England bargains, he was quite honest. In the long run his publishers did well out of him, and this, being a sensible man, he approved of. But the real source of his comfort was the American university world.

He was the great Father Figure of all writers-in-residence. He held professorships at Michigan and Amherst (at the latter he was paid handsomely and continuously for many years, with provision for him to spend the winters in Florida for the good of his health). He did the college lecture circuit until well into his eighties. He gave almost every set of endowed literary lectures at the great universities. He became a kind of American poet laureate, and received more honorary degrees than any writer will ever do again (he professed not to know the exact number, but it was something like fifty: the all-time all-comers' record is Herbert Hoover's 88).

All this would have been destructive to many

* And, after his death, Dylan Thomas.

writers. For him it wasn't. Probably the comfort, nor the money, didn't mean a great deal to him: in those respects he was no more demanding than G. H. Hardy. It was the psychological support he needed. From the colleges, from the students, be breathed it in. Otherwise he wouldn't have gone to them at all. It shows the American universities at their most imaginative that they gave it to him.

Of course, they got a return, and not only from the prestige of having him about. In his lectures, some of the wisdom which distilled from his complex personality kept darting out: and in private he was one of the most interesting talkers about poetry (and, to a lesser extent, about other forms of literature) that I have heard. I felt that when I was over fifty—it must have been even more wonderful, though perhaps even more disconcerting, to listen to as a young man.

Yet there are some teasing paradoxes. No professional writer has ever spent so much time in contact with academic life: and, since he survived to such an age, it will be a long while before any professional writer does so again. But he was not easy with academic literary thinking (he was more comfortable with scientists): and academic literary thinking was not easy with him. On his side, the relation was ambiguous. In his subtle and labile temperament, he was much more academically inclined than he pretended, or liked, to think. His literary originality, though, was different from the originality that the academics of his time were most concerned with. They didn't give him the recognition he longed for: with a few exceptions (Jarrell, Brower) they still haven't done so. Nevertheless, he couldn't tear himself away.

In all his complexities, there was one simplicity. He wanted to write great poems. He was a true artist. As an artist, he had complete integrity. That is, nothing would have persuaded him to write a poem that he knew to be bad. Nothing would permit him to publish a poem with which he wasn't satisfied. In a life longer than Goethe's or Thomas Hardy's, the longest creative life of any poet one can think of, he kept to his own standards. There he was both simple and noble. Somewhere, at the lowest stratum of the shifting quicksands of his nature, there was rock.

That lasted till he died: but so did a rapacity that was never quite satisfied. He wanted to write great poems. He also wanted to be told that he had written great poems. In that, of course, he didn't differ from other writers: but in him, because of his need for reassurance, the desire was unusually strong. He wanted to be recognized on his own terms. Those were definable. They didn't really mean the money, nor the loving audiences, nor the students, nor the honors: these were reassurances, but they were only the fringes of the real thing. His terms were these: he wanted the recognition that T. S. Eliot had received. He knew—he was quite realistic—that he had not had it. He was a very proud man, and an envious one. He did not subdue his envy for Eliot. Eliot had had ultimate recognition, as much as any poet in history. He hadn't. In extreme old age, when he looked a grand patriarchal figure, he preserved a young man's ambition, a young man's rancor, a young man's passion for desires unsatisfied.

It was for this reason that the Nobel Prize meant to him so disproportionately much. He had had plenty of prizes, but this was a symbol. Eliot had won it. He ought to win it. In this he was, for once, unrealistic. If the Nobel Prize had come, it wouldn't have altered the kind of recognition he received: the academics wouldn't have written about him as they did about Eliot: he would still, whatever history says about his work, have been on his own. But passionate men aren't in a mood to appreciate the Philinte-like lessons of literary history. With obsessional intensity, he needed the Nobel Prize: just as, for almost identical reasons, H. G. Wells needed to be an F.R.S.

Of all the passions, envy—the more so when it eats away at large-scale characters—is the least agreeable to contemplate. It is the passion most of us detest bitterly in ourselves. But unluckily it is the occupational disease of much professional life, particularly of the artistic life. The reason is obvious. The criteria of artistic achievement, unlike those of scientific achievement, are not sharp: a creative scientist usually has a reasonable certainty of the value of his work: most writers and painters haven't. I have met one or two writers who judged themselves with inner certainty (I have also met one or two who, with the same inner certainty, thought they were about as good as Shakespeare). But this is relatively uncommon. It certainly wasn't true of Frost.

This uncertainty is responsible for a great deal of the misery, and some of the venom, of the artistic life. Scientists are no more angels than writers, but they haven't the same temptations. It would have been absurd, for instance, for Einstein or G. H. Hardy to envy anyone. Hardy, who was freer from the emotion than any man I have known, used to say, with a sardonic grin, that if Littlewood suddenly produced a proof of Goldbach's theorem,* he (Hardy) would feel murderous for twenty-four hours. That was as far as it went. Einstein, in the second half of his life, was fighting a single-handed intellectual battle against the quantum physicists which bears some formal resemblance to Frost's against the modernist poets: but it wouldn't have occurred to Einstein to regard his opponents as the enemy. Of all professionals, I thought, seeing Frost in great age, still not serene, writers have the hardest job to make themselves good men.

There was one temptation which I wished him free of. He fell into it along with his most illustrious literary "enemies." That is, almost all his life he took up attitudes —they weren't just attitudes, they were savagely felt—of extreme reaction. All through their correspondence Untermeyer, a generous-minded man, argued with him, and at times during the Hitler crises pleaded with him. Frost's replies were as obstinate, and about as well-informed, as those of a Republican small shopkeeper. I don't mean that good writers can't be conservative. Some of the very best have been. But it is hard to make an effort of imaginative comprehension upon a comment like this:

"Friends say to me 'You should side with the poor. Your poems are about the poor.' My answer is I wouldn't have written about them if I had thought anything was going to be done about their poverty. I didn't do it to get rid of the poor. I want them in my business. And anyway when I wrote about them I was poorer than they were."

All one can say is that this is a truer insight (because even here he kept honest to himself), and a more brutal one, into the real core of political reaction than anything

* One of the classical unsolved problems of the theory of numbers.

written by Lawrence, Yeats, Eliot, Pound, Lewis. It is now known where they stood. They prettified or made apocalyptic or classicized their motives. Frost didn't, and to that extent is more respect-worthy. Just as his extreme conservatism, somewhat to the right of Senator Robert Taft, is more respect-worthy than the frenzies of the Action Française or Lawrence's Führer-type rhapsodies. There is, to apply the classical test, no trace of anti-semitism in anything Frost wrote. Still, if his Russian admirers had read his letters, they would have had a shock.

With that said, I should, if I had had the luck, have chosen him for sheer company, after Hardy, of all the people in this book (my third choice would have been Lloyd George). When I met him in England it was at parties, with half-a-dozen people present or more, which would have been a tax on most men of eighty-three, but which didn't seem to worry him. He was expected to perform and did so. He was sharp-tongued, extremely funny, and played on his remarkable gift for having things both ways. In one disquisition he was at his most ambiguous. Two or three of the party were academic critics, and he was baiting them for the symbols that other academic critics—not, of course, themselves, he rubbed in with mischievous courtesy—had read into his poems. He was a simple soul, he explained (did any of them believe it?). When he wrote the word "sleep," he meant sleep. Sleep didn't mean death. He was greatly addicted to sleep. He slept almost any place. Then, playing the other side of the game, he gave what seemed a slumbrous exposition—it was actually pointed—of how his "emblems" (he used the same word as Dickens, and in the same sense) took root in his verse. Emblems rather than symbols. It was a nice academic distinction. It was a beautiful, and entirely conscious, piece of academic analysis.

The next time I saw him was in Berkeley. It was three years later, in November 1960. He had recently suffered his annual disappointment over the Nobel Prize. I had been told that he was, as much as ever, upset. I had arrived for tea at the house of George Stewart and his wife. It was a sunny Californian afternoon: the house was high on the Berkeley slopes, and from the drawing-room window we looked out over the Golden Gate. Frost had been sleeping since lunch, they said. We were having our first drink after tea when he came down. He was still firm-footed, abnormally sturdy for his age. The color of his eyes, I thought, but I may have been fancying it, had faded a little more since I last saw him. He was much less buoyant than he had been in England. For a time we made a little chit chat, some of it about his boyhood in San Francisco—"over there"—getting on for ninety years before. Then with American politeness our hosts made an excuse and left us alone.

He was a deeply subtle man, I knew by now. With such natures it is usually waste of effort to fence: the only way to speak face-to-face is to be direct. I said that I had been waiting for news of the Nobel Prize, and that I was very sorry. He stared at me, and nodded. He didn't pretend not to mind. He said something to the effect that it would be good to have. Then, quite suddenly, he gave a grim chuckle, and launched into an anecdote, possibly apocryphal and certainly slanderous, about another unsuccess-

Robert Frost ⬧ 197

ful candidate—not English-speaking—who had been "bucking for" the prize for years and years. He had left nothing to chance. He had known all the right boys (in Frost's demonology, this probably meant some of the "enemies"). He had been told that it was in the bag. The day of the election, he was sitting with a horde of supporters. He had the champagne out on the table. He was waiting for the telephone to ring. There was a long wait. A longer wait. At last the telephone did ring. He hadn't got it. He was told the name of the winner. "It is impossible!" he cried. It is impossible. It is impossible. That was all he could think of, Frost said, cheering himself up with *Schadenfreude*. But it had happened.

After that, he was quite gay. He talked about England. He was sensitive to his audience, so that I was left under the impression that he had been a life-long Anglophile. When I read his letters and his remarks about "the British," (a term he wouldn't have used to me) I wasn't surprised about some things, but I was by those. Maybe, as I have suggested, he had come to think better of us. He was enthusiastic about the common language—that was the essential thing. Then he spoke about what he called "the locative" in art. Art which meant anything to him was locative, rooted in a place, in the singularities of a place. We had a bit of an argument. Temperamentally, I said, I was on his side. But locative art needs knowledge and patience to understand: that was why cosmopolitan art, abstract art, travelled further and faster. One didn't have to *know* anything to read, say, Kafka or Hemingway. They had travelled round the world to an extent that Jane Austen or Forster never would. Frost wouldn't have it. The greatest locative art transcended everything. It was organic, and no other art could be. He still had immense stamina for argument, or rather for his oblique interpretation of ideas. He would have gone on talking long after our hosts returned.

It was a couple of months after that conversation that he made his greatest appearance as America's national poet. It took place at the inauguration of President Kennedy. In England we saw it on television: we could not tell how cold the day was, though we could guess. It was moving to watch. The old man, standing by the President. The old man who had been through so much, with his vitality still powerful, his insatiable spirit still hungry. He was due to read a poem which he had written for the occasion. In the January sunlight, in the wind, he could not see the print. With extreme quickwittedness on someone's part (quite possibly his own) he began to recite his familiar patriotic poem "The Gift Outright." The slow, unstressed (to English ears) New England voice came out, a little haltingly. At his side, the President's lips were moving, repeating the words he knew by heart.

After that, more honors: the congressional gold medal on his 88th birthday: the triumphant trip to Russia. But still, not the Nobel Prize. In 1962 he was expecting it: but, like the candidate whom he had told me of, the telephone did not ring at the right time. The old passion had not died. But at last his body, though not his struggling nature, had had enough. He was, without much illness, struck by the physical blows of great age—urinary tract obstruction, heart attack, blood clots. It was over in a couple of months. In January 1963, just before his 89th birthday, his old friend Untermeyer went to visit him on his death-bed, the last visit of a lifetime's loyalty. They spoke of the recent triumphs and of what he still wanted. Untermeyer read him a letter from Robert Graves, saying he had proposed him for that year's Nobel Prize. Frost was gratified. He said that he was going to receive another major prize in England in the spring. He told Untermeyer not to forget. "With that hope, I left," wrote Untermeyer. Frost died a week later.

DAG HAMMARSKJÖLD

O NE night in New York, it must have been either in 1959 or 1960, an invitation arrived from Dag Hammarskjöld. It arrived in a somewhat tortuous (and, I thought afterwards, characteristic) fashion. Hammarskjöld was deeply interested and knowledgeable about all the arts, and liked meeting people who practised any of them: one of his deputies, George Ivan Smith, also a very cultivated man, was a friend of his fellow Australian, Sidney Nolan, who was painting in New York and who was a friend of mine. The result of this diplomatic channel was that we were assembled in the morning on the 38th floor of the United Nations Building, Smith, Nolan, my wife and I. I think we vaguely expected to talk to Hammarskjöld about books, which would have been easy for everyone; or alternatively painting, which would have suited everyone but me, and I should have been interested enough not to feel left out. However, it didn't happen quite like that.

Hammarskjöld met us with sparkling courtesy. The

reception room also sparkled, with abstracts round the walls. Showing us to seats on the sofas, he was as immaculate as any man I had ever seen. He was wearing a tawny brown suit, a shade darker than his hair. He had a green tie, and socks exactly matching. I think, though of this I am not quite sure, that he was wearing an American-style white shirt, which he would have been less likely to do in Europe. One almost forgot his physique in the perfection of his attire: but he was long-headed, with Nordic grey-blue eyes, athletically built, about 5 feet 8 or 9. He made an immediate and overwhelmingly strong impression, and the same impression, on the three of us who had not met him. He was the classical narcissist. It didn't need his introspective diary—which was not published till after his death—to tell one this, though he was intensely and sadly aware of it. He made many references to it in his diary. One is: "Narcissus leant over the spring, enthralled by the only man in whose eyes he had ever dared—or been given the chance—to forget himself."

He began to talk. His subject was, believe it or not, the United Nations. All three of us were well-disposed private citizens, and it was a subject in which we were decently, but not infinitely, interested. That did not deter him. He talked with a brittle, tense vivacity. It was a kind of conversation, or rather allocution, which I had not heard before and have not since. I was used to the guarded, Aesopic manner in which high civil servants sometimes discuss their jobs: I had spent years of my life among them, and had learned the language. Perhaps because of that, the most vivacious parts of his discourse were addressed to me. But this was nothing like the talk of high civil servants. Compared with him, they were plain, blunt, brutally outspoken men. His sentences unravelled themselves in impenetrable complexity. His English was as good as ours, but I had to listen, with furrowed concentration, not to what the sentences meant (because that was impossible) but to what conceivable suggestion might, at the end of the Proustian road, lie underneath them.

"Let me be a little indiscreet," he said, the last syllable a little higher-toned than an Englishman would make it—and proceeded to be about as indiscreet as Lord Hankey confronted by someone whom he suspected of being a foreign intelligence agent. And yet, throughout this exercise in the higher incomprehensibility, his manner remained as sparkling, became more so. I have described it as vivacious, but that is not the right word, and for years afterwards I could not decide what the right word was. He gives it himself in his diary—"Coquettish—even in taking note of your coquettishness." That was how he behaved, as he spun metaphysical spider's webs round the United Nations. What was a United Nations "presence?" Could it be possible for the United Nations to be represented in a country without having in fact established, or wishing to establish, a "presence?" Or, alternatively, was there the theoretical possibility that in certain hypothetical circumstances the United Nations could have a "presence," perhaps a symbolic "presence," without being represented in the crude factual sense?

My head spun. This went on quite a long time. It sounds like an unpromising or a farcical meeting. Yes, it was both: but it was also something quite different. For, in the midst of this verbiage, one couldn't help feeling that here was a man crying from great loneliness. Later, comparing our impressions, all of us felt that. I felt something more. I felt exactly as one does when some memory, deep in the past, is struggling to come back to mind. I was liking him, liking him actively, as one likes someone who recalls a person who has been very close. I felt the kind of sympathy I had once felt for someone else. He had, they both had, a special kind of spiritual delicacy. But who was the other? It was like searching for a name which one knows perfectly well but which has been blocked off from one's tongue. The name didn't come back that day, nor for some time afterwards. Then it did. The friend of whom he reminded me was, incredibly, G. H. Hardy.

It seemed absurd. Hardy—the most lucid of men, who believed that unless you could say a thing clearly, you shouldn't say it at all. Hardy, who was not well disposed to men of action, particularly to those who enjoyed their power—which this man did. I did not know then of Hammarskjöld's deep religious beliefs: but they would have made the kinship still more absurd. Hardy would have applied to them the ruthless linguistic analysis of his type of Enlightenment. Hardy, the most extreme of anti-narcissists: compared with the most extreme of narcissists. True—but as I came to think of it, that was close to the spot where their natures met. Somehow those opposite manifestations came from an identical, or at least a similar cause. At the root of their sexual temperaments, they were at one.

It is only too easy to indulge one's psychological fancy. But I believe, trying to be as sceptical as I can, that this is rather more than fancy. I believe further that, if they had met, in spite of all the surface contradictions, they would have understood each other. In a brilliant preface to Hammarskjöld's *Markings* (the introspective diary) Auden remarks that he had "an ego weakened by a 'thorn in the flesh' which convinces him that he can never hope to experience what, for most people, are the two greatest joys earthly life has to offer, either a passionate devotion returned, or a life-long happy marriage." Something of that sort, as I have said, was true also of Hardy, though he took his nature—owing to a piece of luck not granted to Hammarskjöld—more lightly. No one can explain why this should have happened to either of them: in fact, it doesn't rest within our present powers of human "explanation." People have suggested that Hammarskjöld did not become a normal man because of the overpowering personality of his father, who was a great conservative patriarch. I do not believe that these familial and environmental explications stand up to the most ordinary critical analysis. Compared with Hammarskjöld's, in its deepest structure Hardy's temperament was closely similar: but *his* father was a gentle, indulgent, somewhat ineffectual man, with more than a touch of the White Knight about him.

Of the two, Hardy had the better luck. This was due simply to his great specific talent: he was born to be a mathematician, he knew it very early, the realization steered his life, and brought him great happiness. Hammarskjöld had nothing like this source of strength. He possessed almost every intellectual gift (he had a highly competent mathematical mind, great powers of mental

organization, and in addition extreme literary sensibility),
but he was not creative. He might have made himself into
a writer, but he probably wouldn't have been original
enough to justify him to himself.

So there was none of the inner solace of creation,
which to Hardy was more than a solace, which worked
like the spring of organic life. While Hammarskjöld was
still very young, he attained, by the ordinary standards of
the world, great success: this continued without a set-
back: he moved smoothly from lofty job to lofty job,
until, still under fifty, he became one of the major international figures of his time. Some of this he enjoyed, of
course (one mustn't think of his moods, or anyone else's,
as all of a piece), but it wasn't a continuous or permanent
happiness. It didn't work like the spring of organic life.
It didn't lift from him the haunting thoughts of suicide,
which, at the peak of his fame, became transmuted into
something like an obsession with self-immolation or sacrifice.

At 47 (just before he became Secretary-General) he
was writing: "Fatigue dulls the pain, but awakes enticing
thoughts of death. So! *that* is the way in which you are
tempted to accept your loneliness—by making the ultimate escape from life." Five years later: "Do not seek
death. Death will find you. But seek the road which makes
death a fulfilment." Also in 1957: "No choice is unin-
fluenced by the way in which the personality regards its
destiny, and the body its death. In the last analysis, it is
our conception of death which decides our answers to all
the questions that life puts to us. That is why it requires
its proper place and time—if need be, with right of

precedence. Hence, too, the necessity of preparing for it."

It is a somber memento mori that Hardy, when his creative powers had finally left him, also turned his thoughts on death. His taste was too classical, austere and ironic for him to have written anything like those three passages. He took the death-wish with his unadorned candor. But here again, at the end, they were more alike than they seemed: at the deep level they were close together.

Hammarskjöld was unlike the rest of these nine in two particulars. He was the only one of them who was a religious believer (Einstein was a man of strong religious *feeling* but no belief, and that is a quite different thing). As Auden says, Hammarskjöld's diary is an account of an attempt to unite in one existence the active and the contemplative life: the only account of this kind one can remember ever undertaken by a professional man of action, certainly the only account by a man of action as effective and world-famous as Hammarskjöld. This is one of his most interesting aspects, and I shall have a little more to say about it soon.

His second difference from the others in this book lies in his heritage. He was the only one of them, with the exception of Churchill, to be born in the upper-class: and, owing to the dissimilarity between English and Swedish society, his upper-class was radically unlike Churchill's. In fact, there is no precise English equivalent to the Hammarskjöld type of aristocracy. In Sweden there still exists an old aristocracy, descended from feudal grandees: the Hammarskjölds did not belong to that, which apparently has been exclusive for hundreds of years, in a sense that the English aristocracy never was. So that in Sweden there grew up, as far back as the sixteenth century, an upper-class of officials, soldiers, functionaries of the centralized kingdom which had won its struggle with the feudal lords: this "official" aristocracy has persisted to this day, and the Hammarskjölds had belonged to it since 1610. They had held all kinds of high offices of state: his father had, before the first war, been a royal (and somewhat undemocratic) appointee as Prime Minister.

To find anything like an English parallel to this section of society is difficult. It is rather as though the Cecils, who came into notice as civil servants a little before the Hammarskjölds emerged as soldiers, had stayed civil servants and high functionaries for the next four hundred years, instead of merging with, and coming to dominate, the English landed aristocracy. Similarly the Churchills started as soldiers, but after the first Duke became, in the mobile English fashion, enormously rich aristocratic land-owners: so that between the great general and Winston Churchill's father there is no evidence of obsessively conscientious service to the state. In England we have seen families who have produced public servants for three or four generations—such as the Butlers, Barlows, Hankeys —but these have been of comparatively recent origin, just as has been the similar (and connected) development of an intellectual *haute bourgeoisie*, Darwins, Keyneses, Wedgwoods, Hills, Adrians.

One can, however, find "official" aristocracies in other countries, especially in those with a less mobile history. General de Gaulle comes from such a class: so does Peter Kapitsa and other eminent Russians. People with this heritage tend to have characteristic virtues (and also vices, but on the whole the positive side is strong). One is, of course, rectitude: this seems a boring virtue, but unless it is constantly being pumped into society, all goes rotten within a shorter time than most of us would in our youth have believed. Another virtue which De Gaulle, Kapitsa, Hammarskjöld himself, many descendants of lines of high officials, all possess is—courage. And courage of a particular kind. Not careless courage. Courage of the will and conscience. One has been trained to recognize the intolerable. Someone has to put it right. Who more suitable than oneself? If not now, when?

When he was a student at Uppsala, his father was Governor of Uppland, and the family lived in the medieval castle that looks down over the town. For one who, even as a boy, found intimacy so difficult, this can't have helped: nor can it that both at school and university his career was one protracted academic triumph, a whole class above the rest; in fact, a whole class above anyone for years past. This would, I think, have been true at any university; he was not only as clever as a man can reasonably be, but fanatically hard-working (as he stayed all his life). Looking back on my contemporaries at Cambridge —I was born in the same year as Hammarskjöld—I fancy that only Frank Ramsey * could have given him a run. Like most clever men who experienced the university of the twenties, he felt later on that he had been lucky. Rutherford's Cambridge: Franck's Göttingen: Bohr's Copenhagen: there were plenty of stupid undergraduates who

* The best philosophical mind of his time, who died in his twenties. Brother of the present Archbishop of Canterbury.

didn't realize what was going on round them, far more than there would be today, but the universities were at their creative best. It was the same in Uppsala. Hammarskjöld said: "The strange brief idyll which burgeoned all over Europe between two crises and two wars had a reflection all its own in Uppsala."

In the midst of his undergraduate triumphs he was writing aphorisms like this:

Every deed and every relationship is surrounded by an atmosphere of silence. Friendship needs no words—it is solitude delivered from the anguish of loneliness.

To be sure, you have to fence with an unbuttoned foil: but, in the loneliness of yesterday, did you not toy with the idea of poisoning the tip?

Many gifted young men, of course, feel something like that melancholy: some even write it down. The unusual thing with him was, as we now know, that it lasted. What he wrote at twenty is abnormally close to what he wrote at fifty: glittering worldly success made no difference, nor did the passage of time, which usually rubs away some of youth's anguish. The only change in his inner life seems to have been that, some time in middle age, he regained his religious faith.

His worldly success was so smooth that it would have seemed unfair if he had been a happy man. Like some of the best minds in Sweden, he turned to economics, where Wicksell's thinking was having the effect—in actual fact a much more direct and immediate effect—that Keynes's was in England. Hammarskjöld, with his automatic competence, became a good economist: he could have had any academic job: but he wanted the life of action. This was one of the constant themes of his life, and I shall revert to it: but it is quite clear that he went into administration at twenty-five, still working at theoretical economics on the side, because he was determined to arrive at the place where decisions were made: and he was determined to make them. He wanted power. More than most men, he wanted to do good with his power: but power he was going to get. This is somewhat underplayed in his introspective reflections, until it gets interwoven with his religious and sacrificial thoughts. But it was there, deep and strong, when he was quite young.

He got considerable power at the age of 30. Wigforss, one of the ablest Social Democrats in European history, became the Swedish Minister of Finance. He promptly appointed Hammarskjöld to be his top permanent official, the exact equivalent of Permanent Secretary of H. M. Treasury.* In Whitehall this simply could not happen: no one, if he were a blend of Lenin and J. M. Keynes could get the job at such an age: nor at any age could Lenin-Keynes be brought to a top Treasury position from outside the civil service.

The Swedes, very much to their advantage, are more elastic. In Hammarskjöld they got one of the best civil servants on record: he and Wigforss between them, more than any other men, created the Swedish welfare state. It was perhaps an advantage that Hammarskjöld came from a conservative family. It was certainly an advantage that

* To be pedantically exact, there are now two Permanent Secretaries of the Treasury, one of whom presides, as top civil servant, over economic business.

by temperament and conviction he was *dirigiste*. He wasn't a socialist, but it was first nature to him (as it is to all men who want power for what they can do with it) to manage things. Which he did. Which he continued to do when at 36 he became chairman of the Riksbank. (This was something like being Governor of the Bank of England and Permanent Secretary of the Treasury *at the same time*.)

More jobs, leaping upwards—Swedish representative in OEEC at 41, Secretary-General of the Foreign Ministry at 43, non-party member of the Cabinet at 46. He was occupying this last office when he was offered the Secretary-Generalship of the United Nations. He jumped at the job. He had a shrewd idea of what it would mean: he knew that from now on he would live in the public eye: probably, when he did live so, there were more moments of pain than he bargained for: but even if he had known exactly about those moments of pain, he would still have jumped at the job. This was what he wanted. From all kinds of motives, vanity mixed up with nobility. He wanted to leave a mark on history: he had that kind of ambition as strong as most men. He had also, in a subdued fashion, a histrionic streak. He liked being a world-figure. But also he knew that this was his chance to work out his own destiny, to put his faith into action, to do some good.

If he hadn't become Secretary-General, his inner life would have been unhappier, more unsatisfied, even than it was. That is the single point on which I disagree with Auden. He writes: "I do not think that, for a man of Hammarskjöld's temperament, political life was his 'natural' milieu. By training, he was a Civil Servant, that is to say, someone whose job it is to carry out a policy, not decide one. He may, on the basis of his experience and convictions, advise for or against a given policy, but it is for his Minister to decide, and for him to execute that decision. This means that, though he is in public service, he does not enter into the arena of public life and public controversy. . . ."

Auden seems to me to be slightly misreading Hammarskjöld's history, and, for once in his life, to have accepted a stereotype. In fact, at 30 Hammarskjöld must have been making major decisions: top civil servants, in England and probably at least as much in Sweden, always do. I don't know, but I am prepared to bet that it is impossible to disentangle which of the biggest decisions were his Minister's and which Hammarskjöld's. Further, his civil service and public career in Sweden had been mixed up: he was accustomed to being a center of controversy. He had even moved out from all administration to become a Cabinet Minister—that is, a politician—right in the open. I believe that the evidence is conclusive: he wanted, or was impelled to find (what you want is what happens to you, one has to say again), the life of action in its fullest sense, the life of action at its most exposed.

In his diary he wrote, after he had been Secretary-General a couple of years: "In our era, the road to holiness necessarily passes through the world of action."

This is put in his own religious idiom: but if we secularize it, the statement has a deep meaning for many twentieth century men. In our world, can a man feel even remotely reconciled to himself unless he has tried to do what little he can in action? That is a question which has required an answer from many of us: it is part of the condition of modern men. It is, of course, not a new question. Goethe asked it, and so did some Victorian intellectuals. But with them the subjective pressures were stronger than the objective ones. Their moral disquiet came—not entirely but more impellingly—from inside. With us, it is possible to be serene in a private world and yet be forced, perhaps unwillingly, perhaps knowing that we are wasting years of our lives, into the world outside. Malraux was forced in just that way: so was Picasso, so was Einstein. It has meant the rejection of the romantic idea of the artist, such as Frost cherished. But that idea could not genuinely survive into our time. Hammarskjöld was speaking for our time: he knew it better than most.

He knew it so well that he didn't, and couldn't, expect to achieve much at the UN. No doubt he expected to achieve a little more than he actually did: that is a condition for successful activity, or indeed any activity, in any field. As Hardy wrote, one of the first duties of a professor is to exaggerate a little both the importance of his subject and his own importance in it. A man who is always asking, "Is what I do worth while?" and "Am I the right person to do it?" will always be ineffective himself— Hardy went on—and a discouragement to others. Hammarskjöld, despite (or perhaps because of) his inner loneliness, certainly did not ask such questions. Following Hardy's prescription, he exaggerated the importance of the UN by 10 percent. But he knew exactly what he was in for. He had had a long training in the in-fighting of politics (in that particular art, Swedes don't need tuition from anyone on earth). He wrote—and this was before he took his greatest job:

On whatever social level the intrigues are begun and the battle fought, and whatever, in other respects, the circumstances may be, when what is at stake is his own position, even the "best head" unfailingly exhibits his naïvete. The possible tricks are so few. He who pursues such a course becomes as blind and deaf as the cock-capercailzie courting his hen in a fir-tree—especially at these moments when he imagines he is being most astute.

That is written from the inside. And so is this, which could be applied to any human effort, and retrospectively to all he tried to do:

It makes one's heart ache when one sees that a man has staked his soul upon some end, the hopeless imperfection and futility of which is immediately obvious to everyone but himself. But isn't this, after all, merely a matter of degree? Isn't the pathetic grandeur of human existence in some way bound up with the eternal disproportion in this world, when self-delusion is necessary to life, between the honesty of the striving and the nullity of the result? That we all—every one of us—take ourselves seriously is not *merely* ridiculous.

Well, he went through it all. Inner politics, at which he was a master. World-scale politics, where he was on stage ("can there exist a neutral person?"). Suez. The cold war. The Congo. Abuse. Sometimes praise. The story of UN diplomacy over Suez and the Congo is all dead by now. But did the existence of the UN, Hammarskjöld's own existence and actions, make any difference? Without the UN, where should we have been by now? Anywhere else but where we are?

Dag Hammarskjöld 215

It is hard to give a sensible answer. I think I know what my hard-baked military mentors, such as Hankey, would have said. Not by an inch. Since 1945 the world has been governed by power politics. Power politics influenced by a novel technological discontinuity, the nuclear weapon. But power politics similar in kind, though on a world scale, to those of the Thirty Years' War. Those were the facts, and the UN was a debating society. Suez happened to be outside the major power struggle, but, even so, the power factors were constant, it had to come to the same end. If the UN had never existed, the world today would be exactly the same place.

In the short run, this is quite likely true. But it is possible to be too hard-baked about politics. "How many divisions has the Pope?" asked Stalin. He was a realistic man: but that was not a realistic question. How many divisions had Dag Hammarskjöld? He had no power-base, except in the improbable event of the two superpowers agreeing on action, in which case he was not necessary. And yet, as he said of himself, he became a kind of secular Pope. He was not, as people sometimes called him, an international civil servant: the world had not advanced as far as that, there was no world-authority, his staff might be called international civil servants, but he was on his own. He was a symbol: so was his successor, U Thant. They were symbols of a longing for reason in world politics—a longing felt by masses of people in small countries, and by many in great ones. No one can tell how powerful this longing for reason can be, nor whether it can affect state policies. If not, then in terms of action Hammarskjöld was one of the heroic failures. If that

216 **Ν** *Variety of Men*

should be so, then we oughtn't to despair too much. There are plenty of premature hopes which come off in time: and without heroic failures, we shouldn't have many hopes at all.

He would have accepted that. He had extreme courage. He wrote, " 'Courage?' On the level where the only thing that counts is a man's loyalty to himself, the word has no meaning—'Was he brave?'—'No, just logical.' " But he was, in fact, brave beyond the normal human limits. It was, I think, this sense both of virtue and of strangeness which made him admired as a public figure, long before anything was known of his inner life. The public instinct for good heroes is often truer than we think.

A year after Hammarskjöld's death, I was sitting in the same room on the 38th floor of the UN building, calling on U Thant. There could scarcely have been two men more different. The tenseness had all gone: there was no brittle vivacity in the air. U Thant didn't want to give any fireworks display of conversation: we both talked, and we talked in the same terms, sharing many of the same fears and the same kind of difficult hope. He was wise and relaxed. He was as full of goodwill and duty to his fellow human beings as Hammarskjöld, but closer to them, part of the same earth. I fancied then, and still do, that even more than Hammarskjöld, he believed that men, the whole species, all of us, were dangerous wild animals, and that it was going to be a major task for us to save ourselves. Hammarskjöld wrote—"conscious of the reality of evil and the tragedy of the individual life, and conscious, too, of the demand that life be conducted with decency." U Thant, the least hysterical and histrionic of men, was trying to fulfill that last demand: he was ready to spend his life doing so, but with utter calmness he knew how hard it was. To have two such men in succession as symbolic world-figures ought, perhaps, to make us think a little better of our chances.

We are left with the fascination of Hammarskjöld's faith—or what he called his negotiations with himself and with God. This may be the most remarkable thing about him. Through his fifties, to the end of his life, it dominated his inner experience. His mother was a deeply religious woman, and he had been brought up in a climate of fervent evangelical Christianity. For a long time he couldn't believe: then he re-found his faith. At the age of 49 he wrote: "From scholars and clergymen on my mother's side I inherited a belief that, in the very radical sense of the Gospel, all men were equals as children of God, and should be met and treated by us as our masters. . . . I now recognize and endorse, unreservedly, those very beliefs which once were handed down to me . . . . The language of religion is a set of formulas which register a basic spiritual experience. It must not be regarded as describing in terms to be defined in philosophy, the reality which is accessible to our senses and which we can analyze with the tools of logic. I was late in understanding what this meant. When I finally reached that point, the beliefs in which I was once brought up and which, in fact, had given my life direction even while my intellect still challenged their validity were recognized by me as mine in their own right and by my free choice. The explanation of how a man should live a life of active social service in full harmony with himself as a member of the community of the spirit, I found in the writings of those great medieval mystics for whom 'self-surrender' had been the way to self-realisation, and who in 'singleness of mind' and 'inwardness' had found strength to say Yes to every demand which the needs of their neighbors made them face, and to say Yes also to every fate life had in store for them."

There is nothing of the famous Hammarskjöldian ambiguity ("the only man alive who can be totally incomprehensible with complete fluency in four languages," said a baffled diplomat after listening to one of his official explanations) about that declaration. He was clear enough when he was speaking for and to himself. In fact, this declaration was a public one: but, since it concerned his faith, and his justification by faith, it is also clear. Paradoxically, it is almost too clear; that is, it expresses a continuity of faith that he didn't come to without strain and setbacks. There it is, though, perhaps the most unusual testimony by a man of action in our time.

There is no doubt about his search for God, and his certainty that he could not serve his fellow-men unless he did so as the instrument of God. His diaries, for the final ten years, refer to almost nothing else. This was his inner life. It was intensely private and characteristically intense. His reflections upon it are not specially original, less so to my ear than his secular aphorisms. Perhaps he had read too many books: the language of the mystical search tends to repeat itself. Robert Frost, who was not a religious man and who would not have thought of reading the medieval mystics, dug out of himself occasional finds about faith more independent than Hammarskjöld's. The really re-markable thing, though, is that Hammarskjöld was engaged in this search at all—while he was managing, in the world's eyes, great affairs. I cannot think of any comparison: great world figures have sometimes communed with their souls when they have finished acting: but this was done right in the thick of the active life.

One has to imagine him during the Suez period: supremely competent, seventeen or eighteen hours a day in the office, the interminable interviews, the drafting and re-drafting, the multiple negotiations during which he must not make, or even want to make, a straightforward remark, the heart-wearying complex pressure, the detail that can't get simplified, of the twentieth century political existence. Then he went to his lonely flat and wrote:

The last ditch of the enemy. We can sacrifice ourselves completely to that which is beyond and above us—and *still* hope that the memory of our choice shall remain tied to our name or, at least, that future generations should understand why and how we acted. . . . If you do, is it not all too obvious that you are still being influenced in your actions by that vain dead dream about "posterity"?

The question answered itself:

I believe that we should die with decency so that at least decency will survive.

Hallowed be Thy name
    not mine,
Thy kingdom come,
    not mine,
Thy will be done,
    not mine.

Then, next morning, back to the office again, once more supremely competent.

Within his faith, there was an inner mystery. In the quotation above, one of many at the time of Suez, he says, "I believe that we should die with decency. . . ." In the context, the meaning is not apparent: but what he really meant is that some time, in the course of his life of service under God, an actual physical sacrifice would be required. This was not intended metaphorically—he believed, in literal terms, that he would have to take his way along to suffering, shame and the sacrifices of his life. There are many passages which can stand no other reading.

In the old days Death was always one of the party. Now he sits next to me at the dinner-table: I have to make friends with him.

In this intuitive "anamnesis" which has become my Ariadne's thread through life—step by step, day by day—the end is now as real to me as tomorrow morning's foreseen task.

What next? Why ask? Next will come a demand about which you already know all you need to know: that its sole measure is your own strength.

Didst Thou give me this inescapable loneliness so that it would be easier for me to give *Thee* all?

The only value of a life is its content—*for others*.

. . . Therefore, how incredibly great is what I have been given, and how meaningless what I have to "sacrifice".

On the plane of reason, this doesn't make sense. Just how, Auden remarks, did he envisage his end? Did he expect to be assassinated like Count Bernadotte? To be lynched by an infuriated General Assembly? I was distracted by the same puzzle. The Secretary-Generalship of the UN is not a specially dangerous job physically, not much more so than the Archbishopric of Canterbury. It is certainly a job in which a man might reasonably expect to lose some of his reputation. A really worldly man would think several times before accepting it, if he wanted to remain a world-figure afterwards. There are many such jobs, great and small, where the chances of success and increased prestige are worse than even. Hammarskjöld might quite easily have had to leave in something like humiliation. In fact, if he had survived until the full-scale Vietnam war, that would probably have happened. But that is the worst that could have happened. It would mean a psychological wound: but that is ludicrously far away from his dramatic physical forecast of a Way to the Cross.

It looks as though the suppressed histrionic streak in his temperament had, on occasions, got mixed up with his faith: together with the allure of death, of which he wrote himself, describing his experience on mountains:

The arrete that leads to the summit separates two abysses: the pleasure-tinged death-instinct (with perhaps an element of narcissistic masochism) and the animal fear arising from the physical instinct for survival.

When he writes of physical sacrifice, one begins—for the only time in all his introspective passages—to get restive. Yet it is certain that he had a premonition of his own death. In the old term of his Norse ancestors, he was fey. "Fey" is one of the words that have had the meaning taken out of them. It is usually applied to actresses, like Audrey Hepburn, who appear delicate and fanciful. It means nothing of the kind. It means simply that one has foreknowledge that one's death is near. In the greatest of sagas, a character called Ulf the Unwashed makes a remark to his shipmates which suggests that he has this foreknowledge, and they tell him impassively that he is fey: he is duly killed within minutes. Incidentally, it is reasonably long odds against Ulf the Unwashed bearing a marked resemblance, either physically or temperamentally, to Miss Hepburn.

In the exact sense, Hammarskjöld was fey. I don't imagine that most of us would trust such premonitions far. Plenty of people have them and don't die: even more meet sudden death without them. As everyone knows, Hammarskjöld had his premonition and did die—in an aircraft accident on an official mission to the Congo. It could have happened to any politician or civil servant in the line of duty: it doesn't seem much like the sacrifice he had imagined. But, somehow, he has the last word. He might himself have written, as he did in one of his late poems:

> Thou
> Whom I do not comprehend
> But Who hast dedicated me
> To my fate.
> Thou

He had an ironic sense of humor, and he would have enjoyed seeing that read by an unbeliever.

STALIN

A DARK autumn afternoon in the Moscow country-
side. I had not met Leonov before, but I was sitting
in his dacha: outside, the pines and birches, the
haunting, claustral, melancholy Russian scene. The garden
was flowery and trim, more like an English garden than
most Russian ones. It turned out that Leonov was a passionate and scientific horticulturist: like a good many Russian writers, he had an obsessive interest in the natural
world (Nabokov's art derives from the one short dandiacal
and perverse period in Russian literature, but his professional knowledge of butterflies is just what one might expect of his contemporaries in his native land). Leonov was
also involved in cosmogonic theories: almost at once we
were plunged into an argument, and I was grappling, as
I had done so often, with the national passion for abstract
thought. I really wanted to talk about his novels which I
knew well and admired: he wanted to talk about Fred
Hoyle, and his (Leonov's) own original ideas. Still, he was
a most interesting man, inventive and eccentric: if he

225

wanted to argue, he was going to argue: it was some time before we sat down to a meal.

The meal started, I think, about five o'clock. It might have started at almost any other time. I like Russian food and drink: but I viewed this with some caution, for I was due back in Moscow at nine, for more food and drink in Tvardovsky's flat. However, that is the occupational risk of Slavonic travels. If you're prissy, you ought to be somewhere else. So we ate and drank. The sky darkened through the trees outside the dining-room window (it wasn't a large dacha, Leonov and his wife were living there alone, and there were only two largish rooms on the ground floor). Suddenly, for the first time, Leonov began to speak about personal experience. Something in the conversation had reminded him of another dinner, in the Kremlin, in the early thirties, thirty years before. At that time Leonov was already a well-known writer, and he had been summoned to meet Stalin. Whether it was for the first time, I don't remember, and I'm not sure whether he said so: but it was probably the first time that he had met Stalin in an intimate party. It was the kind of party such as has been described by Churchill and Djilas and others. A smallish room in Stalin's private suite. Not more than seven or eight people present (Maxim Gorky was there, but I don't think Leonov told me the other names). A side-table loaded with food—no doubt zakuska, the lavish Russian hors d'oeuvres, and hot courses on warming dishes. No waiters. Plenty to drink: although the evidence is strong that Stalin, unlike a good many of his entourage, was not himself a heavy drinker.

Stalin kept idiosyncratic hours, and Leonov had been invited to come late at night. They sat round a small table, and the interminable toasting went on and on. But Leonov was, not unnaturally, preoccupied with the personality of his host, and, also not unnaturally, with his host's attitude to him. Stalin had been in supreme power for years. He was awesome in the fullest sense. This party happened after the collectivizations, though before the great purges. Leonov was in his mid-thirties, an up-and-coming writer. He felt that, to put it mildly, he was under inspection; and being under inspection by Stalin was not an entirely comfortable experience.

It was a quirk of Stalin's not to sit at the head of the table. He was sitting on Gorky's right hand; saying very little, but fixing each of the party in turn, so Leonov thought, with a yellow-eyed sideways glance. The glances kept falling on Leonov. The conversation was about literature. If he spoke, he was going to attract suspicion. If he didn't speak, he might attract more. Perhaps deliberately, someone began to talk of Dostoevsky. Leonov was known to have been deeply influenced by him: in fact, from Leonov's novels the influence was manifest. Gorky was saying temperately that Dostoevsky had taught the Russian people to accept suffering: in the new society they had to learn to reject it, that was the only way to achieve the full dignity of man. Leonov nerved himself to break in. Yes. Dostoevsky was a reactionary. No one should deny that. But nevertheless Russian writers still needed him and always would.

At once, as though he had been waiting for a signal,

Stalin was leaning across, eyes full on him. Questions barked out. What did he mean? Why did he say that? *What right had he to say that?*

How these questions were actually asked, one can only guess. Leonov was not in a position to act as a detached observer. But whereas western witnesses report that—in the war-time conferences and elsewhere—Stalin might be, and usually was, cold, tough and sardonic, but was always controlled, Russians give a different impression. They insist that often he was excitable and raging with emotion. Certainly that night in the Kremlin Leonov believed himself confronted by passionate suspicion. He was terrified.

Gorky intervened. He was the patron and benefactor of Leonov, and of many writers of his generation. Gorky could speak to Stalin as no one else could, and he did so. No, he said, you are misunderstanding Leonid Leonidovich (Leonov). One need not agree with all he says, but one must respect it. In any case, he has earned the right to speak for Russian writers. Gorky repeated himself (this speech Leonov never forgot) : he has every right to speak for Russian writers.

Apparently Stalin's suspicions died down on the instant. He told Leonov to fill his glass again, clinked it with his own, and drank his health.

Leonov was convinced, thirty years later, that that protective (and typical) gesture of Gorky's saved his life. For he belonged to a literary generation, the first after the revolution, that suffered many deaths in the coming purges. Some of the best talent in the country died, Babel, Pilnyak, Mandelshtam, Koltsov. No, said Leonov, he had no reason to love Stalin. He still could not completely understand the bad times. He had been lucky himself. It would be a long time before anyone could completely understand. It was like living through a plague.

It was really time for me to get back to Moscow. He was still brooding. It had been a terrible time, he said. He had lost friends and colleagues. He might have been killed himself. He had no reason to love Stalin. In a hundred years what will history make of him? The records will be so much of a palimpsest that it will be next door to impossible to write the history: but still, someone will, some time. In that case, said Leonov, he couldn't help imagining that Stalin would seem a great figure. This country has had a dark history, darker than most people in the west even begin to comprehend. Ivan the Terrible, Peter the Great, they were part of the history. Mightn't Stalin take his place beside them?

There are, I have often thought since, some singular features about Leonov's story, some not obvious. It would be unusual, to put it no higher, for an American president or a British Prime Minister to take time off for what was in effect a literary dinner: one of the many singular things about Stalin is that he was much more deeply educated in a literary sense than any contemporary western statesman. By his side, Lloyd George and Churchill were abnormally ill-read, and so was Roosevelt. Churchill in melancholy old age was reading Jane Austen and Trollope for the first time: Stalin, in this like almost all the Soviet leaders down to this day, had mastered the classical Russian literature while he was a student. It is difficult for westerners to realize that in meeting Soviet politicians and scientists they are entering a society better educated in literary (not visual) terms than their own. Stalin's own taste seems to have been solid and serious—though his own taste did not affect what he thought desirable for political purposes. He was presumably interested in Dostoevsky as a political force when he was harrying Djilas. Nearly twenty years later Djilas reports him as saying: "A great writer and a great reactionary. We are not publishing him because he is a bad influence on youth. But—a great writer!" (Since Stalin's death Dostoevsky has been published in enormous editions, and the dramatizations of his works are some of the most popular plays on the contemporary Soviet stage.)

His taste in the theater was even more solid. Some time before the first war, he appears to have attended a performance of the Moscow Art Theatre. This impressed him so much that he wanted the same performance to go on in exactly the same fashion forever. Dramatic authorities in Moscow have told me ruefully that if one of them made mild protests against conservative tendencies at the Moscow Art, he was likely to hear a well-known voice on the telephone the same afternoon asking him what the hell he was suggesting.

It seems a little fantastic that, in addition to Stalin's other activities, he took on those of Supreme Literary Critic. But he actually read the typescripts of most well-known writers before they were published, partly for political reasons but apparently also for sheer interest. The marvel is, how did he find the time. But the evidence is overwhelming. He made neat corrections in green and red pencil. Sholokhov—once again under the patronage of Gorky—was lucky enough to produce *And Quiet Flows the Don* when he was very young, and so avoid this magisterial editorship. But he had much trouble with *Virgin Soil Upturned*. I have never asked him the full story, because I know that this period left a traumatic mark upon him. Sholokhov was, and is, a committed communist (although, as anyone can discover in his art, he has a tragic sense of life). But during the collectivization he was compelled to watch his own people, his own Cossack peasants, sent off into exile, and worse. Sholokhov was twenty-five, but already after Gorky the most famous novelist in Russia. He wrote a passionate letter to Stalin, saying that these were good people, simple peasants, many of them real communists, poor Cossacks. Stalin, who already knew him, as he knew all brilliant writers, wrote back a polite but noncommittal reply. Sholokhov wrote again. This time Stalin replied sarcastically that Sholokhov was a writer who didn't know anything about politics: therefore he had better not waste his time writing letters instead of starting another novel. Sholokhov is a deeply emotional man, as much rooted in the Don country as Faulkner was in Mississippi: his passions are narrow but intense: he cares for his beloved Cossack friends more than for any set of people alive. Not being able to help them in 1930 and 1931 was too much for him: the wound is there still.

Another oddity to western eyes is the close personal relation of political leaders with writers. Gorky was an intimate of Stalin's, and Sholokhov of Khrushchev's. I don't know, but I am prepared to bet that Churchill never met T. S. Eliot except perhaps on a formal occasion. But writers, and the written word, have traditionally been more consequential in Russia than we in the west find it easy to comprehend. That was one of the reasons for Stalin acting as supreme censor. If you believe that the written word affects men's actions, then you watch it. The price for our complete literary liberty in the west is that no one really believes that in terms of action literature matters. Ever since Pushkin, Russians have believed that in terms of action literature matters directly. As a result, writers have had a place in society, and a function, quite different from that of their western counterparts. For that place and function they have had to pay the complementary price, often of suppression, sometimes of death. The writer is a public voice, to an extent we often fail to appreciate at all. At this moment Yevtushenko is a public voice, as Mayakovsky was before him, or Blok, or Pushkin. Vosnesensky is more like a western poet than Yevtushenko: and yet he too is often a public voice. It is probably only the private voices, such as Anna Akhmatova (a beautiful poet), whom the west can totally understand without an imaginative effort: and so we miss the tone of the whole culture.

Just as, incidentally, they often miss the tone of ours. In Tsarist Russia, without any other legal means of opposition, a lot of writers took upon themselves that function. They were the means of protest. Belinsky: Chernyshevsky: Tolstoy: Gorky: they all did work which in our society would be done by politicians. Often Russians find it hard to understand why our writers fail to do such work. They tend, by our standards, to over-rate English writers in whom, rightly or wrongly, they detect a vein of direct social protest. I have had many arguments in literary Moscow, but the hottest-tempered was one day at the Gorky Institute of World Literature. We were sitting round the familiar green baize table, with Ivan Ivanovich Anisimov at the head and young research students far away in the middle distance. Someone mentioned Byron. My wife and I said mildly that we just couldn't regard him as one of the greatest of English poets. Immediately Anisimov (who had a character like a rock and who was a friend of mine) was on his feet, and, following him, his entire staff. It was a little like having one's health drunk. But actually they were all shouting, in thunderous Russian basses: "Here we must disagree with our dear guests. Here there is a complete break between us. . . ."

In the same spirit, they have examined our contemporary literature for signs of social protest (just as incidentally we examine theirs for signs of dissidence) and sometimes think they have found it. It puzzled them that Hemingway (who has had more influence on modern Soviet writing than any westerner) turned out to have no political commitment at all. It puzzled them that some of the writers of the fifties, who seemed to be making protests, were, in practical social terms, doing no such thing. It was then that some of them invented the term—"literature of trivial protest."

Stalin, as I have said, was deeply read in Russian literature and in Russian literary history—and, of course, in Georgian, in which he published his first work, which was, somewhat surprisingly, a poem. He knew, more completely than any westerner, the role of the nineteenth century writers as an unofficial opposition. I suspect he felt, in a way no westerner could, the magical efficacy of literature.

In his struggle for power, he had other forces to look after. But once he had gained power, then this was one among many forces to be looked after: it was not going to endanger either himself or his state.

So, as one might expect, Leonov's attitude to Stalin, fatalistic, reflective, historical, is quite uncharacteristic of other Soviet writers. Most of them, particularly the young, will not grant him anything. Though I do remember an occasion, a year or two later than my talk with Leonov, when we were driving back to Moscow late on a summer night. On the horizon we could see the red star over the university tower—the university block which Stalin had had built out on the Lenin (once the Sparrow) Hills. I was sitting with a man I knew well, a "soldier of the revolution," who had as a youth fought in the Civil War. He said: "I know you don't like that building. I suppose it isn't beautiful. But whenever I see it, I think to myself, damn it, the old devil has done it again."

To set against that, though, there are all the expressions of bitter outrage that I have read and heard. Simonov, writing his savage portrait in the most recent of his war novels: Yevtushenko, sitting in my London flat, reciting *Stalin's Heirs* long before it was published, with all his naked sincerity and considerable voice: scientists, contemptuous and unforgiving—although on the whole they were left alone more than the writers—because Stalin had backed Lysenko and put Soviet biology back for twenty years, and because it took someone as brave as Kapitsa both to rescue Lev Landau (the best Soviet theoretical physicist) and to see that Einstein's physics was not discredited. I should guess that that harsh intellectual unforgivingness is going to last a long time. Simpler souls who marched all the way from Stalingrad to Berlin over their shattered land with its 20,000,000 dead, blame Stalin for the early disasters of the war: the young students blame him for anything they find oppressive.

What was he like? It is already clear that he altered the shape of our lives, not only in his own country but in all of ours, incomparably more than any of the others I am writing about. And yet, even on simple prosaic physical details, it is abnormally hard to arrive at any objective facts. Nearly everyone who met him, his own countrymen or foreigners, saw him through a haze of hero worship, fear or acute hostility. It seems to have prevented them not only reaching any agreement about his nature, but even about his physique. For example, Djilas, who, as a member of Yugoslav missions, spent many hours with him, reports that he had a narrow, short body and disproportionately long legs (he was, like Lenin and most of the first generation of Soviet leaders, a very short man, not more than 5 feet 2). Quaroni, who was Italian Ambassador in Moscow for three years, says with equal confidence that he had a thick, powerful torso and stumpy legs. Which paper do you read?

He was the only one of the subjects of these sketches that I never met. I very much wish I had had the chance. Not that I could have added much: but at least I could have satisfied myself on points like that. And I should have had one small, but perceptible, advantage over most of his interlocutors. I should have been a good deal more disinterested. Of the impressions written by foreigners (there are not many) I am inclined to think that Djilas's is the most reliable. Certainly it shows a sharper eye and ear than any of the others. He records Stalin as saying in 1944, at a time when Roosevelt and Churchill were congratulating themselves on getting on pretty well with Uncle Joe—"Perhaps you think that just because we are the allies of the English we have forgotten who they are and who Churchill is. There's nothing they like better than to trick their allies. During the First World War they constantly tricked the Russians and the French. And Churchill? Churchill is the kind of man who will pick your pocket of a kopek if you don't watch him. Yes, pick your pocket of a kopek! By God, pick your pocket of a kopek! And Roosevelt? Roosevelt is not like that. He dips in his hand only for bigger coins. But Churchill? Churchill—will do it for a kopek."

That sounds authentic. If it isn't, Djilas has considerable talent as a novelist. But he does suffer from two disadvantages which make me hesitate to rely on him as a source. First, and most important, he is a refugee from faith: that is, he had invested all his spiritual hopes in Soviet communism and Stalin himself, and then found that his faith had deserted him. That kind of negative conversion, either in politics or religion, sometimes makes for brilliant art—but not as a rule for objective accuracy. His other disadvantage is a minor but curious one. He seems to have been much too genteel for his company. For a Montenegrin and a partisan soldier, this is unexpected: but he constantly shows himself affronted by the hearty spirit-drinking, the rough, masculine ribbing, which is common form in Russia and very similar (except in small details) to what Englishmen and Americans are used to.

Djilas just couldn't become one of the boys: and this seems to have alienated him, almost from the start.

I said a moment ago that I should have been more disinterested than most of Stalin's interviewers. I had better explain that: for it involves two different things, my feeling towards Russia and towards the Soviet system. I love Russia. I have done so since, as a boy, I became fascinated by Russian literature. Why it had this specific appeal to me, I don't know: but I couldn't resist the mixture of broadnatured realism with the subliminal desire for salvation. Anyway, whatever was the reason, I learned what I could about Russia. When I was still a boy, I learned a simple fact that seemed to escape some of my acquaintances: it was just that Russia didn't begin in 1917. I think that bit of sense has made me keep a fairly level attitude to the Soviet system. I didn't invest as much hope in it as my communist friends did. In the early thirties I was sure—it was obvious enough—that any such concentration of power as was happening under Stalin would bring great dangers: that was the chief intellectual division between me and Bernal. On the other hand, I always wanted the system to develop and work well: and I still do, as strongly as ever. It is foolish to think that western societies have reached the only possible plateau of social organization. Capitalism has proved itself remarkably resilient and adaptable: there are many things it does better than the Soviet system: for example, it will be a long time before a Soviet factory worker, much less a worker on the land, has any approach to the material life of his American counterpart. There are also many things, including impalpable but valuable things, which the Soviet system does better than we do. It is the best hope, though a frail one, for the next generation that we shall learn both the differences and the similarities, and see with clear eyes where we are good and where we are bad.

One can see some of the differences in the first brute fact of Stalin's life. He was born in 1879. His grandfather had been a serf. His father was himself born a chattel-serf, and then became—and this was a step up—a poverty-stricken shoemaker. There haven't been serfs in England since the fourteenth century. The poverty and squalor of his home would make those of Wells or Lloyd George seem indecently opulent. No great political leader in all history has ever come from so deep down in the population. Incidentally, none of the other major figures of the October revolution came from such origins. Lenin's father was an inspector of schools: Trotsky's was a very rare phenomenon, a Jewish landowner. Nearly all the others came from professional families. Stalin alone was born in the depths of the poor. His father was not only an impoverished shoemaker, but an increasingly unsuccessful one. He took to vodka and to ill-treating his son. At a very early age Stalin had to reckon with savage brutality: he learned to be secretive, evasive, enduring, and to keep his mouth shut. It was an awful home, and he learned his lessons well.

He also learned other, and more conventional, lessons well. His mother was a washerwoman: even before her husband died, when the boy was eleven, she was supporting the family. She was patient, illiterate, devoutly religious, and ambitious for her son. Somehow she managed to scrape up, kopek by kopek, the money to send him to an ecclesiastical day school. He was nine years old: he came from a poorer home than anyone there: that must have taught him, not that he needed teaching, what class-privilege meant and what it was like to hate. It was not a bad school, though, except that the lessons were given in Russian, not in his native Georgian. He soon showed that he was exceptionally bright. Later on, there was controversy about his intellectual gifts: I shall come to that a little later. As a boy, it was obvious that he was very clever; he was also proud and not willing to be outfaced. He was one of those children who can't bear not to be Top Boy. He found it wise to hide this desire as he became older. But it was not hidden for ever.

At fifteen he moved on to the Theological Seminary at Tiflis. The ecclesiastical school and the local priest managed to find a scholarship to maintain him there—which demonstrates both that his gifts had been spotted and that his rebelliousness had not been. In fact, his character, like Einstein's at the same age, was already formed, and so were many of his opinions. He was abnormally mature. The main features of the historical Stalin were already set. He was mature enough to do a very difficult thing; that is, to conceal from his teachers and his fellow pupils what he really believed. At sixteen he was in touch with the anti-Tsarist opposition in Tiflis: he wrote Georgian nationalist verses under the first of his pseudonyms: he discovered Marxist circles in the town: and returned to the seminary to sing tunefully in the college chapel.

He kept up this game for nearly five years. Few young men would have that capacity for dissimulation or steely self-restraint. The monks gradually became suspicious, but when they at last expelled him they had not proved—though they suspected—his socialist connections. He had concealed those pretty effectively: but—it was a comic weakness in the precocious master of the underground—he could not conceal his passion for secular literature. Secular literature in the seminary was allowed only if sanctioned by the monks: the circulating libraries of Tiflis were forbidden: Stalin could not resist using one. Not in order to obtain Marxist works, which he got secretly and safely elsewhere, but just to read Gogol, Chekhov, Thackeray, Victor Hugo. He was a compulsive reader, then and later. His fellow pupils, future priests, used to hide books to squint at during the interminable orthodox services. Stalin was better at this art, more obsessively tied to his books, than any of the rest.

He was not yet twenty when he was sacked from the seminary. He was already a professional revolutionary. His short phase of romantic Georgian nationalism was long since over. True, he saw Great Russia, not only with the eyes of the poor, but with the eyes of a minority nation—rather as the young Lloyd George saw England. Georgian was Stalin's first language: his real name was Djugashvili. But, in his hard and sober fashion, he put those romanticisms aside: later on, he identified himself more completely with Great Russia than Lloyd George ever did with England. Nationalist movements were for children: for Stalin, there was the real revolution. It was his vocation. He had precisely one job inside Tsarist society, which he held for eighteen months. It was, rather incongruously, that of clerk at the Tiflis Observatory. It was the only orthodox job of his life until he became, nearly twenty years later, one of the leaders of the Soviet state.

Stalin was not only in the underground, but in the underground of the underground. Unlike Lenin, Kamenev, Zinoviev, nearly all the other aboriginal Bolsheviks, he was never outside Russian territory, except for a few clandestine trips, during one of which he first met Lenin —though he was already a root-and-branch supporter. They were all of them abnegating the present, living in the future, to an extent which most of us cannot enter even in the imagination. The factional disputes, the plans, the incessant debates, the studies in the British Museum— they would all have seemed as pathetic as their nineteenth century predecessors' if history hadn't clicked and the plans come off. It needed inordinate faith and hope, and the passion, or the different passions, which had made them revolutionaries to sustain such a life. And even Lenin, in 1917, two months before February, ten months before October, was telling a group of students in Zurich that he didn't expect to see the revolution in his time but that they certainly would. . . . Yet at least the exiles in Western Europe, denying themselves everything else, had talk, company, ideas. Stalin's life, like that of the other praktiki left in Russia, was much grimmer. It was the deep underground. His colleagues didn't even know his name (at this stage he usually posed as Koba, but there were a dozen other false names). Strikes. Passing on pamphlets. Raids. The bread-and-butter of pre-revolution.

Agents provocateurs. Prisons. Escapes from prisons. Siberia. He got married and, though his wife died young, had a son. He had no sort of home.

Most of the time (more than half the period between 1902 and 1917) he was in prison or Siberia. There—he had to discipline himself to avoid rusting and perhaps, for he too was human, to avoid despair—he set himself programmes of reading. It was from Siberia, beside the Yenisei, that he wrote a completely non-political letter, the only one of his yet published. It was to the mother of the girl who later became his second wife. He thanked the family for their parcels and asked them not to spend any more money on him, since they themselves needed it. All he wanted was *picture postcards:* because where he was, nature in its "dull ugliness" offered nothing to the eyes, except the frozen endlessness of the tundra. "In this accursed country . . . I have been overcome by a silly longing to see some landscapes, be it only on paper."

During his interludes of liberty, he took on, among his other jobs, one which was the most secret of all. The party set up specialized military branches, whose purpose was to train men in guerilla warfare, execute military operations, and bring in money. These military branches were separated from the political organizations: no one knew of them except those who were specifically bound to know. Stalin appears to have been responsible for the staff work, or a good deal of it, in the Caucasus. The secrecy was so extreme that, to this day, his part is not fully known. It is a curious reflection on this century that, in its first decade, these operations caused a *crise-de-*

conscience among the Russian socialists. Thirty-five years later rigidly respectable officers and civil servants of parliamentary democracies were planning exactly the same thing on a gigantic scale, and with the same obsessive secrecy.

The Tsarist police had not the most vestigial hint of Stalin's role. He was the supreme hider of secrets. But once, in a farcical way, the most suspicious of men was not suspicious enough. He had, a few months before, early in 1912, been co-opted by Lenin on to the Central Committee. There was nothing mysterious about his promotion, despite what Trotsky had to say later: I will deal with that controversy shortly. In January 1913 Stalin fulfilled a mission for Lenin in Vienna, and returned to Petersburg. Within a week he had been betrayed to the Okhrana (the Tsarist secret police). On the day of his arrest he attended, of all things, a Bolshevik musical matinee. This was authorized by the police, and Stalin asked a colleague on the Central Committee, Malinovsky, whether it would be safe to attend. Malinovsky assured him that it would be. Stalin was, for once, trusting. Unfortunately, Malinovsky was a police spy.

The farce went further. Lenin tried to arrange for Stalin's escape. The person asked to manage it was, inevitably, Malinovsky. He was not only a member of the Central Committee, but in charge of counter-espionage and the organization of escapes. Stalin was duly despatched to the north of Siberia, from which he wrote that one letter of lament, and instructions from Malinovsky went out to the police. Escape was out. He stayed there until the February revolution. He was suspicious enough already: that episode, when he learned the truth, cannot have made him less so.

Incidentally, the story still seems mildly stupefying. Personal relations at the top of any kind of politics, including revolutionary politics, are usually not at all close: the leading Bolsheviks did not know each other as intimates, any more than members of an English Cabinet normally do: but still, Russians tend to be shrewd psychological observers, and Lenin was as shrewd and attentive as any.

He was certainly shrewd and attentive about Stalin. His name was on Lenin's personnel files very early (from Zurich or London lodging-houses, Lenin ran something like an administration-in-exile), years before they met. At conferences Lenin studied him, and decided that this was a man he wanted. That was the reason why in 1912, at the final break between Bolsheviks and Mensheviks, Lenin put him on the Central Committee. Stalin (he was only just about to be recognized by that name) had been working in underground secrecy. He wasn't much known even to the leaders of the party: people like Trotsky, at that time in opposition to Lenin, regarded his protégé rather as Curzon did Baldwin, as a man of the utmost insignificance. Yet Lenin was a first-class judge of men for functional purposes: like all great handlers of men, he didn't hanker after the unattainable, he made the best of what he had: about Stalin he was, of course, right.

The mists of hagiography have made it harder to see why: so, even more, have the jeers of Trotsky and other enemies. They under-estimated him at the time. They went on under-estimating him. Almost up to the end, they found it inexplicable that he had got anywhere at all. That classical misjudgment tells one something about him, but more about them. Trotsky, for instance, was an orator much more dazzling than Lloyd George and a writer much more brilliant than Churchill: he was arrogant and self-regarding, he took it for granted that a man who didn't possess comparable talents was no good. Stalin was a poor speaker and a flat writer. Trotsky dismissed him, at once and for ever, as a dullard. What was more, Trotsky and almost all the leading revolutionary figures, Bolsheviks and Mensheviks, were eloquent Marxist theoreticians. They talked the theory of the revolution, they wrote it, the subterranean journals were full of it. They despised Stalin because he didn't make theoretical contributions, or even show the capacity to do so.

All this Lenin shrugged off. He may have thought—he had every right to do so—that so far as theory was concerned, he was enough in himself. In fact, nearly all the valuable pre-revolutionary thinking came from him. He had a robust Russian appetite for conceptual discussion, but even he must at times have got tired of argumentative prima donnas. He wanted a practical man: and he had discovered one of the most effective practical men of all time. He wanted someone who knew at first hand what the depths of the Russian population were feeling, what their potentialities were. The others saw the industrial working class, and even more the peasants, as romantically as Russian intellectuals always saw them. No one ever saw anyone, or any group or class, less romantically than Stalin. He had the advantage of his own dark heritage.

Above all, he had realistic judgment. There were two kinds of euphoria swirling round in Lenin's entourage. One was the euphoria of revolutionaries—without which most men, living on nothing but hope year after year, couldn't survive their life at all. The other was the euphoria of exiles—which, as we have all seen often enough since, makes people think that their enemies at home are near collapsing and that victory is cricking its finger. Stalin was singularly free of such euphorias. The tenor of his temperament was on the pessimistic edge of realism. It made him a source of sense and strength.

Lenin had chosen well. No one knows how much time he spent alone with Stalin, or how agreeable he found his company. But Stalin was a loyal and profound admirer, certainly a good listener, probably taciturn himself and occasionally harshly witty. At this stage no one, not even with hindsight, claims to have detected the paranoid streak which developed later. Of Lenin's colleagues, he must have seemed the most solid, hard and sensible, and superficially the most prosaic.

He was like that when, at the age of thirty-seven, he appeared in Petersburg. He materialized, as it were, out of obscurity and exile. It was March 1917. He was still not well known by name, but he was right out of obscurity: for with Lenin still in Switzerland, he was by seniority the acting head of the Bolshevik party. He promptly appointed himself, with Kamenev, editor of *Pravda*.

He may have wished he hadn't, when Lenin arrived three weeks later. His cautiousness, his trace of pessimism, made him hesitate (just as it did at the beginning of the Hitler war): was this the time—yes or no, probably not

—to go all out for the revolution? It needed the deepest insight to see the way through. This Lenin promptly supplied. He supplied it, with a good deal of sarcastic analytical invective, about ten minutes after arriving at the Finland station: adoring colleagues gave him a bouquet and were making rapturous speeches: he didn't want either: bouquet dangling upside-down, he told them what he thought of their shilly-shallying. The next day, at a Bolshevist conference, he delivered himself at greater and bitterer length. *Pravda,* and by implication Stalin (though Lenin was deliberately impersonal, in his own fashion he was educating his followers), did not escape. "It is high time to admit the mistake. . . . Have done with greetings and resolutions! It's time to get down to business." They couldn't seize power overnight. They had to persuade the working people that they had been cheated by the February revolution and wanted a second one. The party must be re-named (this was the moment at which it became the communist party). "Are you afraid to go back on your old memories?"

This was one of the decisive speeches. Stalin accepted it all. In his whole life, Lenin was the only man for whom he felt absolute respect and loyalty. Throughout the rest of that extraordinary and dramatic summer, in each conflict he followed Lenin's line. He showed his usual practical judgment in getting Lenin out of danger when there was a romantic notion on the Central Committee that he ought to give himself up to the Provisional Government. Stalin knew all about contrived assassinations: he stowed Lenin away with the Alliluyevs (whose daughter soon became Stalin's second wife) and then in Finland.

Meanwhile Trotsky had appeared. After the long years of controversy with Lenin, he now joined him. Those were Trotsky's days of glory. As orator, as improvising military organiser, he was at his best. Presumably the smoldering hostility between him and Stalin was, for the time being, damped down. They had other things to think about. They cannot have had any idea that before long they would shortly be engaged in one of the supreme personal duels of all history: though, as I shall say later, it was much more than that.

They were on the same side at the critical meeting of the Central Committee. This happened on October 10, and voted for immediate revolution (which actually took place a fortnight later). The circumstances of the meeting were distinctly bizarre. It took place, for security's sake, in the apartment of one of their opponents, whose wife, a Bolshevik supporter, had got him out of the way. Lenin, emerging from his hiding place in Finland, attended in a wig. The meeting began late at night and went on for many hours. There were twelve men present, and their hostess provided them with tea and sausages. Lenin had a resolution written in a child's exercise book— "That" . . . a long parenthesis, enumerating the favorable conditions, including (1) the support of the majority of the Russian working classes, and (2) the support of proletarian Europe * . . . "the Bolsheviks do now seize power." Kamenev and Zinoviev voted against, the other ten, including Lenin, Stalin and Trotsky, for.

The revolution duly occurred, according to plan. In Petersburg it was over in a few hours, with almost no loss

* This should be noted.

of life. It must have seemed fantastic, even to Lenin, after all the years of living in the future suddenly to have supreme power in one's hands. In fact, he said so. On that same night, he took off his wig behind the ball-room at the Smolny Institute and remarked (rather oddly, in German), "It makes you giddy." Next evening Stalin heard his own name read out as one of the fifteen ministers of the Soviet Government. After the Tiflis Observatory, it was the only job he had ever had. He was not a man given to romantic extravagances: but still, it must have seemed a long way.

Actually he was much more important than one of fifteen ministers. After the revolution, there was an executive of four—he sat on it, together with Lenin and Trotsky. Then during a period of coalition, there was a kind of inner cabinet, where the Bolsheviks had three places out of five. The three places were filled by Lenin, Trotsky and Stalin.

In later years Trotsky was still expressing incredulity at Stalin's rise: and western intellectuals, hypnotized by Trotsky's writing, have wondered how Stalin ever got there. Trotsky they can understand: he was the sort of man of action intellectuals would like to be, particularly if they don't know much about the inside of politics: but Stalin? The question doesn't need answering. The government was faced with civil war: the economy was wrecked: they had some agreeable and attractive figures among them (for example, Lunarcharsky) but very little administrative talent. Stalin was a first-rate administrator, the only one Lenin could rely on. His judgment had been proved by now. He was a master of "closed" politics, most effective in the inner cabinets. It didn't matter that he had none of the public gifts. They were in the tightest of corners, and he was a useful man to have beside one in a tight corner. Of Lenin's colleagues he had emerged as the only man, Trotsky excepted, fit for the highest places.

Trotsky seems genuinely to have gone on despising him. Trotsky was not a good judge of men: in particular, he hadn't a nose for danger, which is one of the most essential of a politician's gifts. He may not even have realized that *this* was the rival, even in their open clashes during the Civil War. The details of those old arguments are not significant. Trotsky was without doubt a great organizer of troops. Stalin possessed, all western observers in the Hitler war agreed, excellent strategic judgment. Somehow Lenin's government—at enormous cost, left with a desolated country, fought over not only by their native enemies, but also by English, American, French, Japanese armies of intervention, which Stalin, like all Russians of his generation and younger, never forgot— won the Civil War. The military arguments between Stalin and Trotsky were buried. But in one way they were significant. They showed that there was going to be an ultimate struggle for power.

While Lenin lived, no one could challenge him. But Stalin wanted power. So did all his colleagues. They wouldn't have lived that life unless they wanted it: that is what politics, not only revolutionary politics, is about. The way in which Stalin attained complete power is a collector's piece of political calculation. It had everything. Gigantic stakes, gigantic risks. Nevertheless, one doesn't understand him or the others if one imagines that they wanted power merely for its own sake. There have been politicians like that, but they are not very interesting, and they don't get very far. The real politicians want power and want to do something with it. That was true of Dag Hammarskjöld. The Bolshevik leaders were hard and ruthless men: like most men of action (with the singular exception of Hammarskjöld, who was a sport) they didn't indulge in introspective examination: but they took it for granted that they, and they alone, could do something with their power. Stalin certainly believed that, with the power, he could save his country and save the revolution. Others believed that, if Stalin were given the power, his policies would ruin both: but that their policies would bring salvation. So those power-struggles were about major issues. They were actually personal, because they went on in a tiny circle, but they were not just about who got the job. It distorts them if we personalize them too much.

There were several major issues. The biggest of them all, which underlay the others, had been breaking through the surface before the revolution. It was an article of faith among nearly all European socialists, and specifically among nearly all Russian socialists, Bolshevik or Menshevik, that though the revolution might begin in Russia, it would not survive unless it spread to Western Europe: and further that, immediately the revolution established itself in Russia, it would in fact spread almost instantaneously, not in a matter of years but of months or weeks. This was devoutly believed by all Stalin's colleagues, even at times by Lenin himself, and most completely by Trotsky. As soon as they had taken power, Trotsky and most of the party intellectuals were—rather like biologists in the time of H. G. Wells—expecting a Second Coming any moment. The Second Coming would be the real revolution, happening in an advanced country, with a skilled and organized working class. (Then this real revolution would, on the side, help Russia out of its primitiveness— but that was a secondary consideration.) The country Trotsky and the others were looking to was Germany. After Germany, the rest. Some of their successors were still, so strong was the faith, expecting a communist revolution in Germany almost up to the Second World War.

One ought to remember that the Russian revolutionary emigres knew Germany very well. In fact, they knew it better than their own country. Some of them were curiously ignorant about their own country, and hadn't much hope for it. Whereas Germany—there you could really build a revolutionary society. Germany had been the great educator of Eastern Europe (Russian education to this day shows many Teutonic influences). It had the biggest, best-disciplined and most progressive proletariat in Europe. Whatever happened in Russia, in Germany all would come right.

Almost alone, Stalin doubted all this. He doubted it before the revolution, and he doubted it more sardonically afterwards. He didn't know Western Europe as well as the others; his visits, added together, amounted to only a few weeks: but all his hard suspiciousness was at work. He was also, as usual, more harshly realistic than his colleagues. He understood better than they did the power concentrated in the authorities of a highly organized state (he was later to demonstrate what centralized power could mean). He didn't believe that the German proletariat would ever fight against that power. He knew Russia as the emigres didn't: he had no illusions: he knew how backward it was: but for once he had some faith.

Anyway, in his view Russia would have to look after itself. No one would save it. The Soviet system had to survive in Russia, or die there. The country was on its own. This view he expounded, in guarded terms, well before the revolution. He could not make it explicit at any time: but there is no doubt that this formed the inner consistency of his career. As he grew older, he became more certain that no advanced society would have a revolution. Centralized state power was growing more invulnerable every year. He also seems to have been impressed by the adaptability of capitalist structures. His original judgment had been correct.

This judgment—or perhaps more exactly this insight —gave him a single-minded strength. Between his detailed policies and those of his rivals, there was a good deal of overlapping. They all agreed that Russia had to be built, even those who were most hopefully looking over their shoulders at Germany. They all agreed that the industrialization of Russia had to be pushed on. As a consequence, some development and collectivization of agriculture had to follow—just to free workers for industry. Many of these steps were forced. There are, of course, far sharper limits on political decisions than people used to think. Even in a dictatorship many of the choices aren't genuine choices, they are compelled, and would have to be made in a similar fashion whoever was making them. Stalin's originality was in degree rather than kind. "Socialism in one country" was a sharper formula than anyone else's: just as his concept of the speed of industrialization was more extreme. The country had to be forced into a modern industrialized state in half a generation: otherwise it would go under. Whatever else he did, in this he was manifestly right.

He didn't make those absolute decisions until the power-struggles had been won. To begin with, during most of Lenin's lifetime, Stalin played it cool. Unobtrusively he got the party apparatus into his hands, while the others either didn't notice what he was doing or thought that this was the kind of routine administrative job he was fitted for. Stalin knew better. He got hold of the party's personnel machine. He realized that anyone who controlled personnel controlled a remarkable amount of the state. Appointments, promotions, demotions—whoever had those files on his desk possessed real power. This was not a new discovery: nor was it a discovery that could only be made in a revolutionary society. English Prime Ministers made it quite a long time ago: so did English civil servants. In a quiet and apparently amateur manner, Treasury bosses have been studying files about junior colleagues ever since the civil service became a professional corps. I recollect in the late forties having to ring up a civil service friend—who has since become an eminent boss himself—about an appointment which concerned us both. I mentioned the Treasury. Over the telephone his voice dropped to a reverential whisper. "They know a *frightful* lot about one," he said. Well, Stalin came to know a frightful lot about the up-and-coming figures in the communist party.

There was Trotsky. When he was playing against this surreptitious master, did he ever stand a chance? It is difficult to believe that he did. He was, as I have hinted, an intellectual's politician, not a politician's. He was arrogant, he was a wonderful phrase-maker, he was good at points of dramatic action. But, as with Churchill (there are some resemblances), his judgment, over most of his career, tended to be brilliantly wrong. In politics, particularly in the life-and-death politics of revolution, you can't afford to be brilliantly wrong. He had opposed Lenin on most issues during the years before 1917. His colleagues hadn't forgotten that anti-Bolshevik past. Further, he was liable to sway himself with his own eloquence. He wrote that the English working class, after the First World War, were far to the left of the I.L.P. He must have believed it: but it was about as sensible as saying that the English working class in the sixties was far to the left of Frank Cousins. It was the kind of miscalculation that the Soviets could not afford. He was a brave and dashing extemporizer: but when it came to steady administrative policies, he could suddenly swing into a bureaucratic rigidity stiffer than any of the others'.

Above all, he hadn't the animal instinct that a politician needs. When Lenin died, he was convalescing in the Crimea. He didn't return to Moscow. He did not obey one of the oldest of political rules: never be too proud to be present. In a time of crisis, the first essential is to be on the spot, in physical presence, in the flesh.

No, I don't believe he could ever have made it. If by a fluke he had done, he wouldn't have lasted long. Stalin was leaving nothing to chance. He made an alliance with

Kamenev and Zinoviev to keep out Trotsky: just as, shortly afterwards, he made an alliance with Bukharin and the right wing to keep out Kamenev and Zinoviev. It was accomplished political chess. At this time (the mid-twenties) the penalties for being out-maneuvered were no greater than in an English Cabinet: it was ten years later before the paranoiac horrors set in. I ought to repeat the warning that I gave earlier. The maneuvers were so claustrophobically dramatic that they tempt one to personalize the arguments too much. They were about real things: about nothing less than how to run a great, ramshackle, muddled country.

Trotsky was certain to fail: but could anything have stopped Stalin making it? That is a genuinely interesting question. The answer seems to be—nothing but the direct intervention of Lenin himself. There are indications that Lenin, in the last year of his life, was getting uneasy about Stalin and his accumulation of power. But Lenin was a very ill man. He had had serious strokes, though he was still in his early fifties. He had been struck down so young that he had not had time to prepare for the succession. With ordinary luck he would have had ten or twenty years to rule himself. Of his leading colleagues, a good many were highly intelligent men, and some very attractive: but there were few who could possibly run a modern state. Stalin and Trotsky were the only two who had high executive ability. Trotsky was out: Lenin couldn't conceivably have backed him. Which left Stalin.

If Lenin had been in charge for another ten years, he could have trained a new group of rulers. If he had lived in adequate health, even for one more year, he might have arranged some sort of condominium. He had tried to invent administrative devices which would check Stalin's control over the party. The truth was, there were no automatic and built-in safeguards within the Soviet state (this was a result of the dangerous optimism of the communist founding fathers). It has been stated that Lenin finally reached the point of deciding to take drastic action against Stalin: the complete truth of the story will have to await future historians. Anyway, Lenin had his third stroke, at the age of 52, in March 1928. He lingered on for nine months: but now Stalin was secure.

Stalin got the full power, the absolute and complete mastery of the Soviet Union, by 1929. He had continued to play the right against the left, both ends against the middle, the middle against each end. Almost to the last, when Bukharin was desperately trying to patch up an alliance with Trotsky, they all continued to underestimate Stalin. In personal terms, his victory was still quite civilized. Trotsky was sent into exile. At that time, it was unthinkable that anyone should be killed. Several of Stalin's opponents were given good jobs and were close to the government.

At once he started (and was partly driven into, for some of these processes were inevitable, which is one reason why his enemies were so weak) the greatest of all industrial revolutions. "Socialism in one country" had to work. Russia had to do in a decade something like what England had done in two hundred years. It was going to mean that everything went into heavy industry. The primitive accumulation of capital wouldn't leave much more than subsistence for the workers. It was going to mean an effort such as no country had ever made. Yet in this he was dead right. Even now, in the 1960's, one can see traces of the primitive darkness from which the country had to be yanked—side by side with technology as advanced as any in the world. Stalin's realism was harsh and unillusioned. He said, after the first two years of industrialization, when people were pleading with him to go slower because the country couldn't stand it:

To slacken the pace would mean to lag behind: and those who lag behind are beaten. We do not want to be beaten. No, we don't want to be. (Old Russia) . . . was ceaselessly beaten for her backwardness. She was beaten by the Mongol khans, she was beaten by Turkish beys, she was beaten by the Swedish feudal lords, she was beaten by Polish-Lithuanian pans, she was beaten by Anglo-French capitalists, she was beaten by Japanese barons, she was beaten by all—for her backwardness. For military backwardness, for cultural backwardness, for political backwardness, for industrial backwardness, for agricultural backwardness. She was beaten because to beat her was profitable and went unpunished. You remember the words of the pre-revolutionary poet: "Thou are poor and thou art plentiful, thou art mighty and thou are helpless, Mother Russia."

We are fifty or a hundred years behind the advanced countries. We must make good the lag in ten years. Either we do it or they crush us.

At this date, no person of moderate detachment could disagree. Industrialization by itself meant hardship, suffering, but not mass horrors. The bitter problem arose with the collectivization of agriculture. To carry out any great industrialization needs more food for the towns and less workers on the land. Peasant agriculture isn't adequate. In England we had been lucky. Our agricultural revolution, or system of agricultural improvement (which included enclosures, so dark in the history books and folk memory, and yet in the long run necessary), preceded the industrial revolution. It was usually easy to feed the increasing industrial population.

In the Soviet Union the two processes had to go on in the same months, in the same two or three years. With horrifying human losses. An entire class of rich peasants (the kulaks, who were farmers employing paid laborers) was wiped out. Millions of poor peasants, including some of Sholokhov's Cossacks, starved and died. It is hard to write about it in cool and abstract terms. Stalin himself told Churchill that it was worse—not in terms of lives but of responsibility—than the Hitler war, but that it was inevitable. Was it? It is difficult not to admit that some sort of collectivization was, in fact, forced by events. The old Russian peasant agriculture was, by western standards, medieval, something like the English agriculture of the fourteenth century. Further, the Soviet Union, lucky in everything else that nature can offer, is perceptibly unlucky, both geographically and geologically, in growing soil. This is its one great inherent disadvantage compared with the United States. So, executed with the most accomplished skill and humanity, collectivization would not have been easy. It was actually executed about as badly as it could be: and contemporary Russia is still paying some of the price.

Many loyal communists were afflicted at the time. There is a story that the horrors of the collectivization were responsible for the suicide of Stalin's second wife.

Stalin ✻ 259

But, despite his remark to Churchill, it is almost certainly wrong to imagine that Stalin felt it as a personal suffering. Men of action, even those who possess strains of kindness which no one discovered in him, are not made like that. If they were, they would not be men of action. Decisions involving thousands or millions of lives are taken without emotion—or, to use a more exact technical word, without affect. This was true of Asquith, an unusually amiable man, presiding over the Somme offensive in 1916: or of Churchill in the second war: or of Truman signing the order to use the atomic bomb.

Men of action may, and often do, cry easy: but they don't lose sleep and they don't worry. If you worry, I once heard a leading English statesman say, himself responsible for some hair-raising decisions, you oughtn't to be doing the job. These homicidal decisions are taken by men capable of, to use one more technical term, horizontal fission. They act: and the rest of their mind is at rest. It might be better if men weren't constituted like that. But they are. When Stalin was talking to Churchill, it is a fair bet that he was thinking of his activities with comfort: they had made Russia strong: his industry had proved strong enough for the war: his armies were beating Hitler's: his country would emerge as the second great power of the world.

In those conversations Stalin sounded like a completely rational, if completely ruthless, leader. That was how Churchill accepted him—as differing only in the scale of ruthlessness, not in its kind, from other pantocrators. Over part of his career this is, without serious doubt, true: and this was the basis on which, Leonov was suggesting, history might ultimately judge him. But there was an aspect, both before and after the war, in which he differed from other pantocrators: in which, far from being completely rational, he seems to have been paranoiac: in which he inflicted grotesque suffering on his own country, particularly on its most gifted people, and incidentally darkened political hope the world over, for a generation.

The one certain fact about the great purges—which meant the death of tens of thousands and the imprisonment of many times more *—was that they happened. They began to happen in 1935, when he had total power, and went on to 1939: they were resumed again, some time after the war, and continued till his death. It is possible to construct two types of explanation. The first doesn't involve any kind of psychologizing. I should say that, in general, I am against psychologizing about historical figures unless one is driven to it. It is too facile, and the psychological imagination, even when rigidly controlled, is a weapon that can lead one into silliness. Nevertheless, I should say at once that I cannot accept, at least not without qualifications that partly transform it, the first explanation.

It is this. Stalin was, as we know, an abnormally suspicious, but also a sane and rational man. He had, by 1934, just succeeded, not in making the Soviet Union strong, but in putting it in the way to being so. We now know, more than we did, about the morphology of revolution. At precisely the same interval, seventeen years after the outbreak, another revolution, the Chinese, start-

* These figures are only estimates.

ing from different roots, in a quite different culture, ran into acute internal conflicts. Stalin had the identical experience. He was rational but impersonally merciless. He was determined that his regime—and of course his personal position—should remain intact. He knew the dangers of autocratic rule. Externally he was faced by the prospect, not the probability but the certainty, of imminent war. He knew as much about conspiracies as any man alive. Conspiracies were likely to happen—in the party, in the army. He had presided over secret revolutionary organizations, the secretest of the secret, thirty years before. The only counter to secret organizations was the secret police. He was prepared to use, he did use, the secret police as no one had used it before. He would eradicate, he did eradicate, any possibility of an alternative government, not only rivals, but the shadows of rivals, the remotest ambience from which another administration could come. With those measures he, the regime, the country, survived the war. After the war, there was no resting space at all. He had to look at America armed with atomic bombs. Once more the regime must be protected. The same techniques. The same secrecy. The same sacrifices, if necessary, of the innocent: just so long as there was nobody who could be a focus of danger.

Some of this analysis cannot be dismissed. It seems not impossible that Tukhachevsky and other high army officers had in 1937 made a plot to depose him. In fact, it is a priori likely. With such a concentration of power, and with no legitimate instrument of change (this was both the tragedy and the warning of the Stalin era, and it was both foreseeable and foreseen), the army became the only alternative. This was a lesson which Roman autocrats learned a long time before, and it was acted upon by men comparatively balanced, so far as we can judge, such as Septimius Severus and Constantine. There has been plenty of homicide round most autocracies.

As well as military conspiracies, vestigial civilian ones may have been talked about. Trotsky, from exile, was certainly trying to stimulate an opposition. Yet none of this removes the evidence of active paranoia in the central figure. Stalin wouldn't be the first or only person with persecution-mania to have something to feel persecuted about. For my part, I cannot resist the conclusion that, from his middle fifties, he was subject to persecution-mania, certainly to an extent which went a long way beyond reason, and possibly at times, more dominatingly at the end of his life, so far beyond reason as to come within a clinical definition.* I find myself taking something like Leonov's view of his stature as a historical figure. I have no doubt that both his ability, and his direct share in the Soviet Union's emergence from paralytic weakness, have been absurdly under-rated. But I believe that he became a paranoiac. Unlike most paranoiacs, he could act his delusions out. There was no means of holding him.

The evidence is cumulative and convergent. In his young manhood, right up to the days of supreme power, no one suggested—not even Trotsky, who, however, like Churchill, was not interested in psychological detail—anything particularly unusual about him. Maybe he was abnormally watchful and suspicious: but professional poli-

* I am, however, far from satisfied as to how we can draw such a line, either with him or with anyone else.

ticians have enough reason to be suspicious, and, as we have seen in the episode of Malinovsky, sometimes he wasn't suspicious enough. The accounts of his behavior are reconcilable with a paranoid streak—but that kind of paranoid streak we meet among some of our acquaintances every week of our lives. These acquaintances are usually not among our favorites, at least when we have grown up: paranoid personalities take but don't give, and we're wise if we don't have close relations with them. But still they can and do lead socially acceptable lives. They are usually, in my experience at any rate, rather happy.

Stalin may have lived, with consummate effectiveness, in that state until he maneuvered himself into the supreme power, and as a consequence ran into supreme danger. He had been a pretty secret operator. He had exposed himself to open power and vulnerability. The combination may have pushed him near the edge.

Certainly the impressions of his personality in the mid-thirties and later tell of a sharp-edged change—not exactly of a different man, but of a transmogrification. Khrushchev is not, of course, a disinterested witness: but his stories of Stalin's questions: "Why are your eyes so shifty today?" "Why are you turning so much today and avoiding looking me directly in the eyes?" sound unlikely to be pure inventions. The more so, as they coincide closely with anecdotes, written or oral, of so many others, less partial but also speaking at first hand or close second hand.

It is true that western observers in the Hitler war, meeting Stalin for the first time, found an impassive, harsh, magisterial statesman. But one ought to remember two things. First, paranoia can and does co-exist with complete rationality at other levels, in fact at all levels when the root of persecution is not touched. Stalin could remain a masterly strategist and administrator on all subjects which didn't impinge on the delusional system. Just as I have myself known a young scientist who did high-class original research at the same time as believing that he was being persecuted by the entire Royal family.

Second, it is sensible to wonder whether the records have been correctly interpreted. When Churchill took the news that there was to be no second front in 1942, he had a rough reception: but Stalin that night seemed to be placated, almost delighted, by the promise of the landing in North Africa. The next night, however, he started off with a bitter low-voiced storm of suspicion and abuse. Churchill and his advisers drew the conclusion that Stalin was acting under instructions, that these dramatic sun-and-shadow changes of mood were dictated by persons and forces behind and beyond Stalin, whom the western intelligences could never identify, but who held most of the power.

At the time this seemed wildly improbable: we now know that it was sheer fancy. There were no such persons, Stalin held all the power. It would have been better for Russia, and for all of us, if the Churchill interpretation had been true. But isn't it much more plausible to assume that Stalin was behaving according to the character later revealed to us by his own entourage? Paranoia flickers in and out like sexual jealousy. Like sexual jealousy, it is, on the immediate moment, very easily placated—and, just as easily and with increased bite, it returns. On the first night he was being given the guarantee of the North African landings. This was better than nothing. To his military eye it looked a good idea, and he wasn't being quite let down. Then hours of brooding. The suspicions hardened. Wasn't this after all simply a device for putting off the second front, not just for months, but for years? Wasn't Russia, wasn't the system, being left to suffer? As usual, the suspicion wasn't by any means baseless. But his rage next night wasn't merely a statesman's impersonal, rational, bargaining rage: it had the special, gritty, paranoiac force from the root of his nature.

That is a speculation, but it meets the facts better than the present version. Nevertheless, it wouldn't be worth making if there were not the darkest of historical facts. The purges happened. If they hadn't happened, no one would be speculating about Stalin's nature, certainly not I. As they did happen, both in their quality and quantity, there we have the final evidence. As I say, people have searched for an explanation in terms of purely rational motives. I do not believe that it can stand up. Let us put on one side the mass horrors, the camps full of hundreds of thousands of anonymous Solzhenitsyns. It is enough to concentrate on simpler and more comprehensible facts. In the first purges, there suffered:

All the members of Lenin's Politburo (except Trotsky, who was in exile, and Stalin himself):

The Chief of the General Staff, the Chief Political Commissar of the army, the Supreme Commanders of all important military districts:

90 percent of Soviet Ambassadors:

25 percent of the officer corps of the army (this is an estimate, but probably on the low side):

1108 out of 1966 of delegates to the 17th Party Congress held in 1934 (i.e., delegates selected by Stalin's own personnel machine):

98 out of 139 of members of the Central Committee elected at the 17th Party Congress:

The two chiefs of the secret police (Yagoda and Yezhov) —who had produced the evidence for the trials of all the rest

Those facts, at the same time terrible and grotesque, call out for an explanation. None seems admissible which does not include an element of paranoia in the executant.

Finally, his last, King Lear-like years. For most of his behavior we have as yet no information except that supplied by Khrushchev, who had every temptation to overstate his case. It is certain that Voznesensky, the chief economic planner, was killed: it is certain that the chief figures in Leningrad, who had been the organizers in the great siege, were killed. We do not know whether the old members of the Politburo, Molotov, Mikoyan, Voroshilov, were, as Khrushchev insisted, in danger of their lives. But we have one stark piece of testimony, his own revelation of "the doctors' plot": and that is difficult to regard as sane. In January 1953 it was announced that nine professors of medicine, the official doctors to the Kremlin, had been discovered to be in the pay of the American and British secret services. They had already murdered two party leaders and were planning to assassinate the highest figures in the army. Six or seven of the doctors were Jewish, and were accused of acting under orders from an international Jewish organization.

It was a lunatic web of persecution, like the pictures that paranoiacs often draw. Stalin died before the doctors could be killed, and the first act of the post-Stalin regime was to vindicate them. It was lucky that he died in time. For otherwise there would have been another series of purges, with Jews the victims. At last they had entered explicitly into his delusional system. In his earlier years he had shown no signs of personal anti-semitism: it would have been impossible for one brought up on Marx and Lenin. True, some of his enemies, Trotsky, Kamenev, Zinoviev, were Jewish. But so were a high proportion of the original revolutionaries. So was Kaganovich, who was a life-long supporter. Stalin knew better than anyone the primitive anti-semitism of the illiterate peasants from whom he sprang, the anti-semitism endemic through Russian history. But it was only towards the end, when the remnants of training, ideology, reason itself had snapped, that he came to share it himself.

"He found Russia working with a wooden plough and left her equipped with atomic piles": that is Deutscher's famous epitaph, though he went on to add that the epoch of the wooden plough was still lingering persistently on all too many levels of the national existence. Something like that will have to be said in all future epitaphs. But there will be left the tragedy and the questions. Why did he become paranoiac? It was obviously induced, increased to the nth power, by position and danger: perhaps, if he had remained a private citizen, he would have lived out his life muttering dark suspicions, inventing reasons why he had not got on. But there must have been something intrinsic in his nature.

What it was, we have no analytical techniques to tell us. Einstein quite early in his life got interested in psychoanalysis: but, though he kept a deep respect for Freud, he decided that the concepts would have to be re-formed, the emotive words replaced by more abtract formulations, before the subject could be anything but a pre-science. One feels that the more strongly when one runs into Freud's theory of paranoia: "Persecutory paranoia is the means by which a person defends himself against a homosexual impulse which has become too powerful." In any sense in which words are rationally meaningful, those aren't. I knew Richard Aldington well for many years. His homosexual impulses were negligible. He loved women devotedly and passionately: it was the main theme of his existence. He was paranoiac to something like the extent that Stalin was. There was a break in our friendship because, without doing anything at all or saying a word, I found that I was part of a conspiracy against him. We were, I am glad to say, reconciled before he died. In the same way, in any meaningful sense Stalin's sexual composition isn't relevant: so far as that went, he was a normal man. If we are going to reach the roots of his abnormality (or Aldington's), we have to find quite different means of exploration, and of those we are not yet in sight.

The more practical question is, how does a society give power to its leaders, and at the same time make sure that it can be controlled? In the cruellest form, this was the problem, and the insoluble problem, of the Stalin era. But it is also a problem, though a lesser one, in parliamentary systems like ours or that of the United States. By necessity, by the increased centralization of a highly articulated state, an English Prime Minister, and much more an American president, has been given power which would have been unthinkable in the nineteenth century. It is true that, in theory, we have erected, as a result of the historical process, a set of checks-and-balances which ought to, and usually does, avoid the grosser dangers. Nevertheless, we have had at least three examples of men in the highest positions who weren't fit to make decisive choices, but who were left in place. One was Woodrow Wilson, for a couple of years: another was Roosevelt, for his last few months: another was Churchill, for his last year. No great harm was done, for the degrees of freedom at Yalta would have been small, even if Roosevelt had been in his prime. Yet harm could have been done. It is enough to make us reflect. What would happen if an American president suddenly became unbalanced? It wouldn't be long, of course, before he was quietly put into hospital: but it doesn't take long, in the modern world, to have quite considerable effects.

Wooden ploughs to atomic piles. The dark history of Stalin. The triumphant emergence of Russia. The hideous cost to a generation. The wonder, at least to me, is that human beings can be so resilient. Many Russians, contemporaries of mine, have known civil war, Stalin, the Hitler war, experiences which to us are unimaginable. Yet they warm one with the illimitable Russian hope. Some of the darkness, of course, they can't forget: but then they look to their children, and their children's future. As a friend of mine said, discussing his own life, and talking of his sons: "They have known nothing of all this. They are so pure."